Ultimate Microservices with Go

Combine the Power of Microservices with Go to Build Highly Scalable, Maintainable, and Efficient Systems

Nir Shtein

www.orangeava.com

First published: April 2024

Published by: Orange Education Pvt Ltd, AVA™

Address: 9, Daryaganj, Delhi, 110002, India

275 New North Road Islington Suite 1314 London,

N1 7AA, United Kingdom

ISBN: 978-81-97223-98-3

www.orangeava.com

Dedicated To

My Beloved Mom:

Anat Shtein

All the People Who Supported Me Along the Way

To You, Dear Reader, for Making This Journey Worthwhile

About the Author

Nir Shtein is a multifaceted engineer, lecturer, public speaker, and author with a deep focus on open-source software (OSS), Kubernetes, Golang, DevOps, and backend engineering. He has imparted his knowledge through lectures, articles, and podcasts and has held various leadership positions, including Academy Lecturer, Tech Lead, Team Lead, and Software Engineer.

Throughout his career, Nir has transitioned from working in large corporations to dynamic early-stage startups, embraced academic roles, and developed distinctive open-source projects. He has been an active participant in Accelerate programs, further enriching his professional experience.

Over the years, Nir has delivered lectures on an international scale and authored several articles that have reached a global audience. He has contributed to numerous OSS projects, with his most successful project amassing over 100,000 users.

In addition to his professional achievements, Nir has mentored many individuals, guiding them into the high-tech industry and helping them to kickstart their careers. Beyond work, he enjoys reading, listening to podcasts, engaging in sports, cooking, and exploring new places, constantly seeking new experiences and knowledge.

About the Technical Reviewers

Noopur Tanwar is a professional in Software Development, specializing in backend development and mobile app development, with a focus on Microservices. She has worked in various industries such as automobiles, telecommunications, retail, and transport. With expertise in languages such as Java, Kotlin, and Golang, Noopur possesses a strong understanding of their technical concepts and idiomatic coding practices. Her experience in software development could provide insights into how technology is portrayed in literature.

Currently, Noopur works as a Senior Backend Developer in Golang at Quest Global, where she is working on developing APIs for the Jio App. Her work contributes towards making code more readable, maintainable, scalable, and reliable across the organization. Noopur's passion lies in writing code that is not only functional but also solve problems efficiently and elegantly. This passion drives her to constantly strive for improvement, to meticulously refine every piece of code she works on, and to explore new technologies and methodologies.

Gaurav Arora is a Microsoft MVP award recipient. He serves as a Mentor of Change with AIM NITI Aayog, Government of India, and as a Business Coach with Business Blaster, Government of NCT of Delhi. Additionally, he is a lifetime member of the Computer Society of India (CSI) and serves as an advisory member and senior mentor at IndiaMentor. Gaurav is certified as a Scrum trainer and coach, ITIL-F certified, and PRINCE-F and PRINCE-P certified. He is also an open-source developer and contributes to the Microsoft TechNet community. Gaurav has authored books across various technologies and has recently been recognized as a world record holder for writing books on exceptional technologies.

Acknowledgements

Writing *Ultimate Microservices with Go* has been an incredible journey, and I owe immense gratitude to the individuals who have been instrumental in making this book a reality. This project could not have been achieved without the steadfast support, wisdom, and expertise graciously provided by so many.

Firstly, I would like to thank everyone involved in writing this book in one way or another. I discussed the content of this book with colleagues, employees, friends, and managers–people who mainly supported me in sharing my knowledge and leveraging it into this book. Special thanks to the technical reviewers, whose thorough assessments and valuable feedback significantly improved the book. Their commitment and knowledge were crucial in polishing the content and guaranteeing its precision.

I am grateful for the constant support from my family. A special acknowledgment goes to my mother, Anat Shtein, whose encouragement and understanding have strengthened me during this writing journey. I also extend heartfelt thanks to my father, Ron Shtein, for his unwavering support throughout this project.

Lastly, thank you, the readers, for selecting this book as your guide on this learning journey.

Preface

Welcome to a fantastic journey through the world of microservices architecture with the Go programming language. This book is intended for developers looking to broaden their understanding and grasp the bigger picture of microservices. It emphasizes the importance of holistic comprehension over specific technical details, especially in an era when AI can automate many simple tasks.

The objective is to provide a panoramic view of microservices architecture and its practical applications rather than diving into every detail. The aim of the book is to equip you with the foundational knowledge and skills to develop robust services in Go, architect scalable systems, and ensure their successful deployment to production.

Throughout this book, we will explore the essentials of Go programming, delve into advanced topics, and navigate the complexities of building and deploying microservices. We will emphasize the strong connection between microservices, Go, RESTful APIs, and Kubernetes, covering key areas such as service communication, API design, container orchestration, security, and observability.

By the end of this journey, you will have a solid grasp of architecting and implementing microservices using Go, preparing you to tackle the challenges of efficiently bringing your services to production. This book is not just a guide but a stepping stone to continue developing your skillset and exploring new horizons in the ever-evolving world of software development.

Chapter 1. Introduction to Microservices: The chapter explores the evolution of microservices from alternative architectures, highlighting their benefits and drawbacks. We also examine the rising popularity of microservices and the synergy between Go and microservices, showcasing how Go's simplicity and efficiency complement microservice-based applications.

Chapter 2. Usability of Go: The chapter delves into the reasons behind Go's creation, its core principles, and the typical experience of a Go developer. We explore Go's simplicity, minimalist design, suitability for cloud environments, maintainability, and ease of transitioning from onboarding to production. Additionally, we'll examine Go's vibrant ecosystem, including its communities and extensive support network.

Chapter 3. Go Essentials: The chapter equips you with the essential knowledge and tools necessary to become proficient in the Go programming language.

Chapter 4. Embarking on the Go Journey: The chapter delves deeper into Go's advanced topics and principles, building upon the essentials previously covered. We will explore a few Go best practices, techniques, generics, and contexts.

Chapter 5. Unlocking Go's Concurrency Power: The chapter continues our exploration of advanced Go topics by unlocking the language's powerful concurrency features. We'll delve into the world of Goroutines and Channels. Additionally, we'll cover the Pub/Sub pattern, Channel Closing Principle, strategies for avoiding Goroutine leaks, and more.

Chapter 6. Core Elements of Microservices: The chapter dives into the core components of microservices architecture, shedding light on the elements that transform a standard architecture into a microservices-oriented one.

Chapter 7. Building RESTful API: The chapter delves deeper into the development of RESTful APIs, building on the foundations laid in the previous chapter. We'll start with an overview of the RESTful approach and its constraints. We'll discuss essential API capabilities using Go, including documentation, versioning, caching, and so on.

Chapter 8. Introduction to Kubernetes: The chapter introduces Kubernetes, providing developers with the basic tools and knowledge to work effectively with this powerful container orchestration platform.

Chapter 9. Deploying to Production: This chapter focuses on safely delivering production services from a developer's perspective rather than the operational side. We'll explore the challenges and obstacles developers face during the deployment process.

Chapter 10. Next Steps in Production: This chapter addresses the crucial phase after deploying your application to production: maintaining the service and managing potential failures. We'll explore strategies for monitoring and ensuring observability, utilizing logs, metrics, and tracing to gain insights into the system's behavior.

It is advised not to stop here and strive to learn and gain more knowledge. Today, it is essential to keep learning and discovering new topics and tools because the software industry is moving at breakneck speed.

Happy reading and continuous learning!

Get a Free eBook

We hope you are enjoying your recently purchased book! Your feedback is incredibly valuable to us, and to all other readers looking for great books.

If you found this book helpful or enjoyable, we would truly appreciate it, if you could take a moment to leave a short review with a 5 star rating on Amazon. It helps us grow, and lets other readers discover our books.

As a thank you, we would love to send you a free digital copy of this book, and a **30%** discount code on your next cart value on our official websites:

www.orangeava.com

www.orangeava.in (For Indian Subcontinent)

☑ **Here's how:**

Leave a review for the book on Amazon.

Take a screenshot of your review, and send an email to **info@orangeava.com** (it can be just the confirmation screen).

Once, we receive your screenshot, we will send you the digital file, within 24 hours.

Thank you so much for your support – it means a lot to us!

Downloading the code bundles and colored images

Please follow the links or scan the QR codes to download the ***Code Bundles and Images*** of the book:

https://github.com/OrangeAVA/Ultimate-Microservices-with-Go

The code bundles and images of the book are also hosted on ***https://rebrand.ly/bprpy51***

In case there's an update to the code, it will be updated on the existing GitHub repository.

Errata

We take immense pride in our work at **Orange Education Pvt Ltd,** and follow best practices to ensure the accuracy of our content to provide an indulging reading experience to our subscribers. Our readers are our mirrors, and we use their inputs to reflect and improve upon human errors, if any, that may have occurred during the publishing processes involved. To let us maintain the quality and help us reach out to any readers who might be having difficulties due to any unforeseen errors, please write to us at :

errata@orangeava.com

Your support, suggestions, and feedback are highly appreciated.

DID YOU KNOW

Did you know that Orange Education Pvt Ltd offers eBook versions of every book published, with PDF and ePub files available? You can upgrade to the eBook version at **www.orangeava.com** and as a print book customer, you are entitled to a discount on the eBook copy. Get in touch with us at: **info@orangeava.com** for more details.

At **www.orangeava.com**, you can also read a collection of free technical articles, sign up for a range of free newsletters, and receive exclusive discounts and offers on AVA™ Books and eBooks.

PIRACY

If you come across any illegal copies of our works in any form on the internet, we would be grateful if you would provide us with the location address or website name. Please contact us at **info@orangeava.com** with a link to the material.

ARE YOU INTERESTED IN AUTHORING WITH US?

If there is a topic that you have expertise in, and you are interested in either writing or contributing to a book, please write to us at **business@orangeava.com**. We are on a journey to help developers and tech professionals to gain insights on the present technological advancements and innovations happening across the globe and build a community that believes Knowledge is best acquired by sharing and learning with others. Please reach out to us to learn what our audience demands and how you can be part of this educational reform. We also welcome ideas from tech experts and help them build learning and development content for their domains.

REVIEWS

Please leave a review. Once you have read and used this book, why not leave a review on the site that you purchased it from? Potential readers can then see and use your unbiased opinion to make purchase decisions. We at Orange Education would love to know what you think about our products, and our authors can learn from your feedback. Thank you!

For more information about Orange Education, please visit **www.orangeava.com**.

Table of Contents

CHAPTER 1
Introduction to Microservices

Introduction

In this chapter, we will explore the world of microservices, a revolutionary architectural style that has transformed how we build and deploy software in the modern era. Microservices offer a granular approach to software development, where applications are broken down into smaller, independent services, each responsible for a specific function. This modular structure promotes agility, scalability, and resilience, enabling organizations to adapt to changing market demands and technological advancements rapidly.

During this chapter and throughout the book, we will overview the trends and coupled relations of the two major topics of this book: Microservices architecture and the Golang programming language. We will see their strong correlation, why it happens, and how.

This chapter will provide a concise overview of the contemporary method used in constructing architectures–the microservices architect. We will compare it to other architectures, and we will see when it is beneficial to use this architecture and when Microservices create adverse effects.

Structure

In this chapter, we will discuss the following topics:

- Brief History of Microservices
- Monolithic, SOA, and Serverless
- Benefits of Microservices
- Drawbacks of Microservices
- Popularity of Microservices

- Popularity of Golang
- Combination of Go and Microservices

Brief History of Microservices

Let's start by saying that many people claim they have the right to invent the microservices architecture. According to Wikipedia, the first person who mentioned something similar to microservices was Fred George in 2004. He worked on architecture that he called "*Bayesian Principles*". In 2005, Peter Rodgers introduced the term "Micro-Web services" at the Web Services Edge conference. Many individuals can claim that they invented it because there isn't a clear definition of a microservices architecture. Since then, many people have presented things that look like or feel like microservices. It is important not to confuse between microservices and SOA, which we will later detail the difference between them. Since then, its popularity increased over the years and accelerated between 2014 and 2015 (*Figure 1.1*).

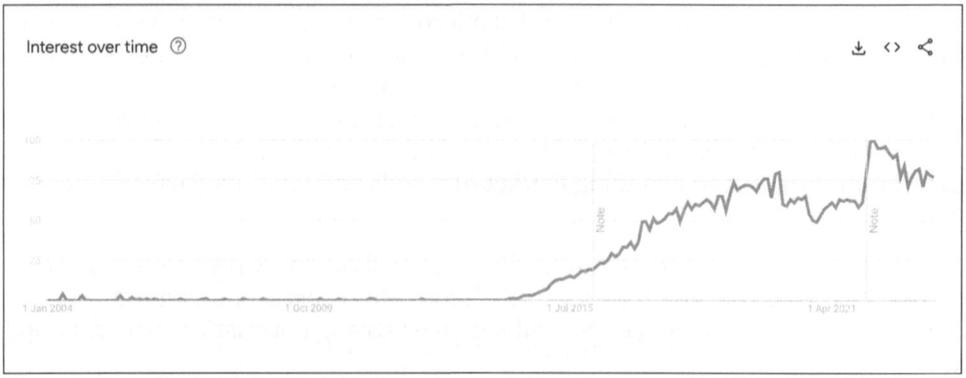

Figure 1.1: *Microservices searches over the web by Google Trends*

A note on Google Analytics: This is a great free online tool. It can primarily be utilized for entertainment, as observing trends is fascinating. It is highly valued for exploring subjects and aggregating information.

Monolithic, SOA, and Serverless

It is helpful to know the other alternatives to some terms or technologies to have a clear understanding of them. The common architecture styles used for a while from the early days of the software industry are Monolithic, "*Service-Oriented Architects,*" aka SOA, and some other architecture we won't elaborate on in this book.

Monolithic

"*Mono*" from ancient Greek means solo, single. As the name suggests, this architecture is structured as a single block of code deployed on a single platform. Usually, in a monolith architecture, there are three main parts - storage (DB), web app with client-side, and backend that acts as server-side, which contains all the business logic, data layer, and everything (*Figure* 1.2).

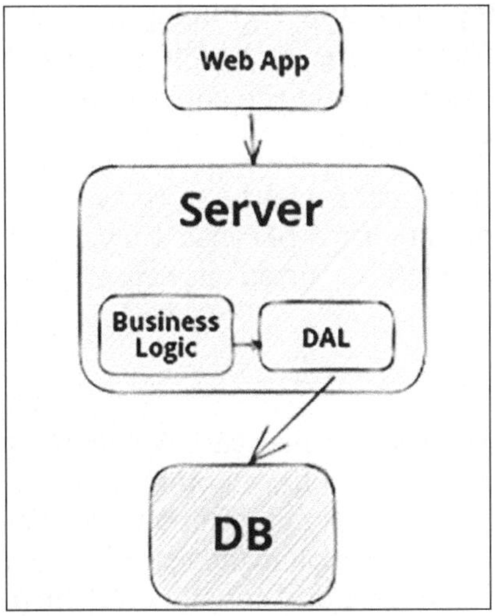

Figure 1.2: *Simple Monolith Structure*

DAL is an acronym for Data Access Layer. This software middleware is responsible for giving software layers that have direct access to the DB and provide tools like retries, error handling, cache, and so on.

As we can see from the simple diagram, this architecture is straightforward. However, all the components are strongly interdependent.

In a nutshell, these are the pros and cons of a monolith:

Pros

- Simple to develop and simple to deliver to production.
- Minimum amount of hops: No need to communicate between one service to another, and we can save a lot of time by decreasing the latency, which leads to better performance.
- Very easy to implement the DRY principle (don't repeat yourself) – due to the single codebase.

Cons

- **Spaghetti code**: As the codebase is extending, the code has more potential to be cumbersome.
- **Harder to troubleshoot and debug**: Navigating a large codebase can be challenging. Even harder to find a malicious bug that caused a side effect in a hidden function somewhere.

- **IDE**: The integrated development environment (IDE) is overwhelmed. Note that there is an approach for writing microservices in a Monorepo, a single repository for all the services.
- **Easy to gain legacy code and technologies**: We are afraid to change core functionalities, infrastructure, and technologies in a large codebase. These changes can dramatically affect the application because keeping old code and old technologies is convenient.

Nowadays, microservices architecture is the most famous in the market, and people tend to reject monolith architecture because they think it is outdated. However, Monolith architecture can benefit in various use cases.

SOA

SOA stands for Service-Oriented Architecture. While the name might be misleading compared to microservices, they do have commonalities. However, there are a lot of differences between them. SOA is an architectural style that organizes software systems as a collection of loosely coupled and reusable services. In SOA architecture, there are two main parts - providers and consumers. The provider and consumer can be on the same deployable component/application/server. This is the significant difference between SOA and microservices. This approach was developed in the early 90s. In those times, the operation part of software engineering was more intricate. We had specialized teams focused on infrastructure, security, databases, and so on.

We would place the SOA architecture between the monolith architecture and the microservices architecture at the decomposition level. Monolithic architecture behaves as a single unit, while microservices architecture behaves as a fine-grained division.

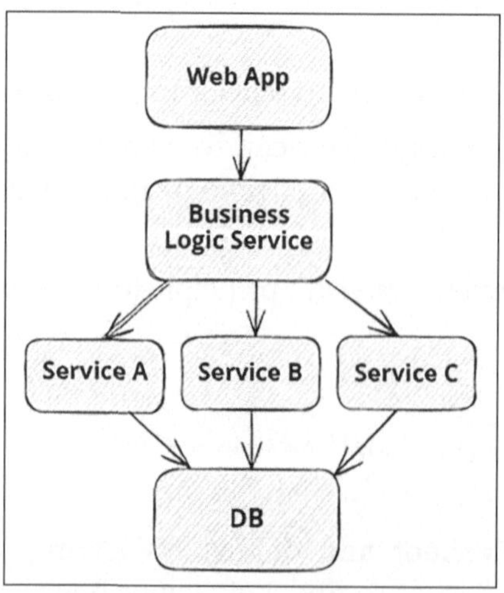

Figure 1.3: *Simple SOA Structure*

In a nutshell, these are the pros and cons of SOA:

Pros

- **Reusability**: Reusability is the core of this approach. It allows us to separate concerns at the service/API level and reuse infrastructure, such as hardware, network, OS, and more.
- **Separation of concerns**: It isn't fine-grained as microservices. Still, it allows us to parallel and deliver our service/API without depending on other teams.

Cons

- **Side effects**: Issues in shared components can affect other components. For example, if the consumer or provider consumes too many resources, if some environment variables change, or any other side effects, all of these can easily affect all existing services.
- **Performance Overhead**: The additional layers of abstraction and communication protocols in SOA can introduce performance overhead. Service invocations across different components and networks may cause latency, potentially impacting response times, and overall system performance. The concerns of network issues are also the same concerns for DBs.
- **Complexity** : Implementing SOA can introduce complexity to our services.

Serverless

This architectural approach is the most modern architecture from the ones we presented here.

Naturally, the cloud's creation led to a serverless architect's creation. The core of this approach is to extract infrastructure concerns and leave us with doing the things that matter - business logic. As the name implies, this is "server" + "less" - meaning no server exists. Of course, there is infrastructure and a server somewhere that runs the code. But we are not responsible for managing this server. The cloud vendor is responsible for all that work. Examples of such technologies are the Functions service of GCP or Lambda of AWS. And many more services/products aim to support the serverless architecture.

Before examining the pros and cons of serverless architecture, we want to discuss two core concepts: FaaS and Bass.

- **FaaS**: Stands for functions as a service. We write our function/API endpoint and let the cloud do all the other work.
- **BaaS** : Stands for backend as a service. We can concentrate solely on developing and maintaining the clients and not on storage, database management, networking, and other infrastructure aspects.

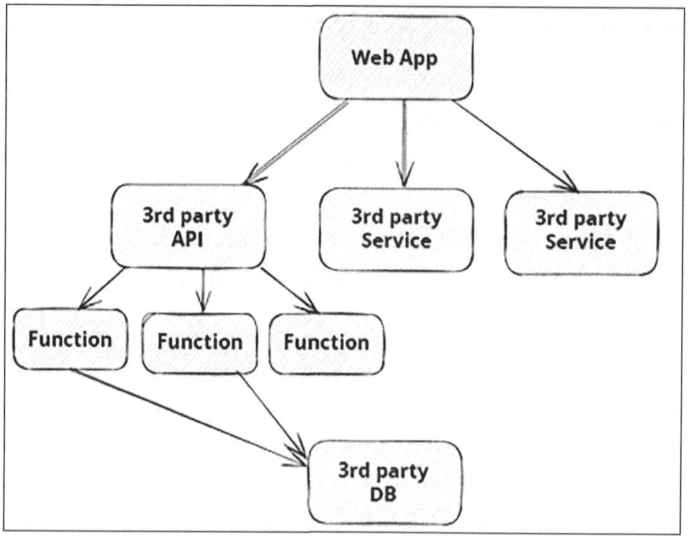

Figure 1.4: *Simple Serverless Structure*

As we can see from the diagram, we, as developers, only wrote the green blocks (Function), and the cloud vendor provided all the yellow blocks (third-party service/DB).

Pros

- **Highly efficient development process**: The development process is highly efficient, with rapid initial development. Infrastructure concerns are no longer a burden, as the serverless architecture seamlessly manages them.
- **Easy to scale**: The scaling process is very straightforward - the only things we should worry about are the resources a function uses.

Cons

- **Vendor lock**: Once we use a specific vendor, all the configurations and settings are specifically for our services. Transferring to another vendor can be very painful.
- **Edge cases**: There are some scenarios when we want to do something but can't due to the limitations of the vendor services that we use.
- **Monitoring**: Since we rely on the vendor to take care of the infrastructure, we also need to rely upon him to provide monitoring tools or integrate other SaaS/OSS monitoring tools.

The cost of serverless architecture is controversial. In serverless architecture, we pay per usage, usually for CPU and memory. We have a lean billing model, and the method of using it is simple. More than that, it goes without saying that we save money on fewer DevOps, operations, and infrastructure engineers. However, other opinions say doing these things ourselves will save money, arguing that we don't have the flexibility to utilize our specific architecture and operation.

Benefits of Microservices

The following figure generally describes how microservices look, and we already can see the difference between this architecture and the other architectures.

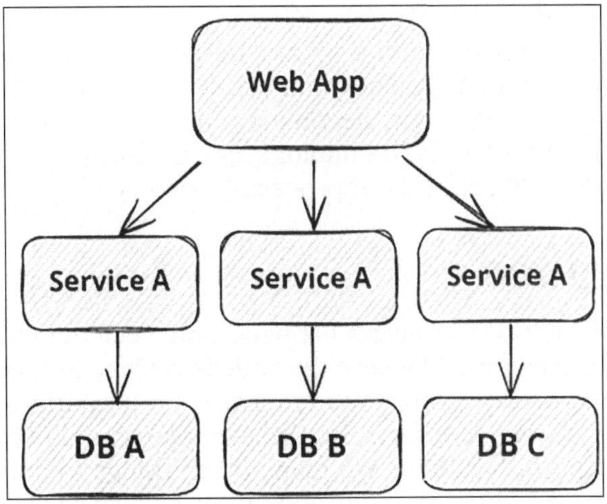

Figure 1.5: *Simple Microservices Structure*

Independent Workloads

By design, microservices architecture splits the architecture into separated services/ APIs/ components. These services are delivered and packaged individually within self-contained deployable units. The self-contained units principle is one of the significant differences between SOA and microservices. The separation of many workloads decreases the size of the codebase, which leads to more minor services.

Minor services mean lean binary, fast build, and so on. Another significant effect is that each workload doesn't affect other workloads. We know the dependencies in advance, and this makes it effortless to deliver services as containers. Containerization is the best practice when it comes to microservices. Both of These concepts deliver the same goal–separation of concerns.

Since the codebase is divided per service, there is no shared code (usually). Each team can work independently on its code without disrupting other teams. A separated codebase leads to breakneck initial development speed. Another effect is that each team can test its services without considering other teams' services.

Easy to Scale

Let's start by talking about vertical scale (scale up). Vertical scale means adding more resources (bigger machines). However, there isn't always a direct correlation between resource consumption and the ability of the service to handle more load. Microservices architecture has become much more helpful when we want to perform horizontal scale (scale out). It is seamless to perform scale-out, just increasing the number of replicated machines/containers for the wanted machine.

Plug and Play

An exciting way to look at microservices is as a honeycomb structure. Each bee builds its cell. It is also elementary to replace one cell with another. The ability to replace a service with another service can become handy when we want to remodel our architecture, experiment with new technologies, or perform some tests in the current architecture. Also, the rollback/rollout processes become simple and easy.

Fault Tolerance

Failure is a typical scenario that always happens, and we should be prepared for this. We aren't living in a perfect world where the code is perfect and the server has a 100% success rate. The microservices architecture made this preparation easier because of the loose coupling between the services. Each service can fail without affecting the other services. Also note that there are many other things to consider when talking about failure (retries, graceful shutdown, and more), and we will talk about that. But at least microservices set a ground base to handle failure properly without considering other services, making the work easier.

Increase Agility

In a nutshell, Agile - is the ability to work fast and to be flexible. There is a vast theory and techniques regarding how to be Agile, and we'll discuss it further in this book.

Each service has its codebase. A team can be responsible for one or more services without relying on or depending on other teams, which is a crucial capability for working with the Agile methodology. Also, when a new member joins the team, onboarding becomes effortless. They don't need to learn all the service codes, only the services their team is responsible for.

Drawbacks of Microservices

Here are the drawbacks of microservices:

Operations Overheads

As we discussed before, the primary benefit of microservices is that each workload/deployment is independent and delivered separately from other services. We saw all the enormous advantages of this. But there is another side to the coin. To allow each service to deliver as a separate deployment, we need to support it from the operation side.

There are many things to consider for each service – service configuration, packaging, separate tests, separate deliverable units, and so on. These examples emphasize that working with microservices requires much operation work compared to monolith or SOA.

Complexity

Naturally, with the increase in services and workloads comes the complexity of managing them all. The previous drawback of operation overhead is that it is just a specific use case of the complexity of microservices. Also, managing data and consistency becomes harder – the data is distributed among each service because each service has its database.

Each team can write its services using its favorite or most relevant programming language. This ability has benefits and disadvantages. The operation must create, maintain, and tackle operations issues for all these programming languages.

Moreover, switching developers between teams will be harder when each service is written in other programming languages.

It isn't a coincidence that we chose to write in this book about Kubernetes and how we will deploy the microservices architect on Kubernetes and not on other platform/s. The primary reason is that Kubernetes is coming to solve this complexity problem.

Hard to Troubleshoot

It is a continuation of the previous point. Due to the complexity of microservices, it is harder to gain visibility above it and create full observability. Many obstacles prevent us from reaching good visibility.

Popularity of Microservices

Various trends happened that led microservices to be so popular.

The first and oldest of them is the Agile methodology. Although it is a pretty old methodology, Agile gained popularity merely when the Agile Manifesto was published (there is a link to it in the references). We highly recommend reading it; it exists in many languages and is very simple to read. Note that it doesn't contain actual practices such as Scrum and Kanban. The Agile Manifesto is considered the doctrine of the Agile methodology.

The Agile Manifesto makes us fast and flexible, so the microservices approach suits those reasons. It is easier and faster to deliver small software than one big piece, which the microservices architect allows us to do.

The cloud computing industry is the second trend after the Agile Manifesto. The leading cloud vendor, AWS, launched in 2002. And from there, this is history; nowadays, using cloud computing is the go-to for many companies and projects.

As we mentioned before, one of the significant disadvantages of using microservices architecture is the operations overhead that comes with it. In my opinion, this is the main reason why microservices weren't prevalent before. The ROI (aka for range of investment) was not worth it! Cloud computing technologies have made our lives much more straightforward in many ways, but the major one is the operations area. So suddenly, building microservices architecture using cloud computing resources sounds like a good ROI.

The next trend we want to look at is the Docker Engine.

Generally, containerization was invented long before docker. Docker was a critical player that led us to use containerization; nowadays, it is so easy and accessible. Docker was launched in 2013 and was very popular right away. *Figure* 1.6 shows Docker searches trend by Google Trends:

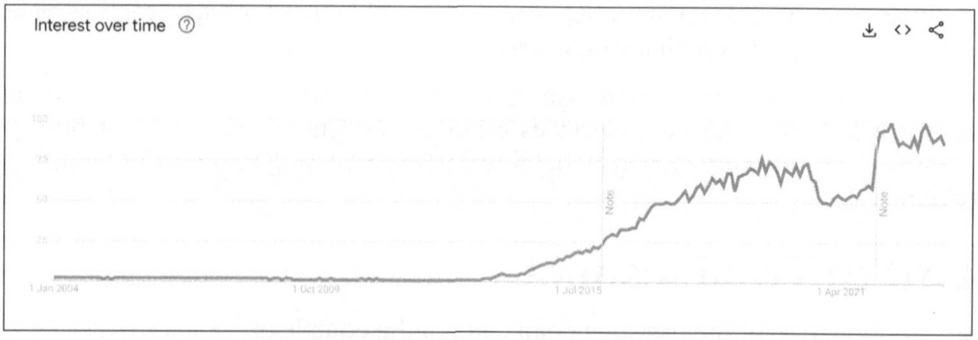

***Figure 1.6**: Docker searches over the web by Google Trends*

One of the core benefits of microservices is that they can deliver independent workloads/deployment. Docker aims to deliver software as isolated containers. Microservices aim to deliver isolated software, and no matter how, running containers using the docker engine is perfect.

The last trend we want to talk about is DevOps methodology. It is weird to call it methodology, but this is what it is. Nowadays, it has become a job title. There are also very similar jobs that do similar things, such as SRE, Production Engineer, and more. Again, as we mentioned before, the major drawback of microservices is the operations overhead. The DevOps methodology comes to solve it, or at least to decrease it.

Popularity of Golang

A metric we can follow to see the popularity of Go is the increase in Golang users–developers, or we should call them Gophers. The nickname for Golang developers is Gophers. The gopher is an animal that counts as the official mascot of the Golang programming language. Here is a friendly dashboard from StackOverflow insights where we can see the percentage of developers who want to learn Golang and become professional developers in Go.

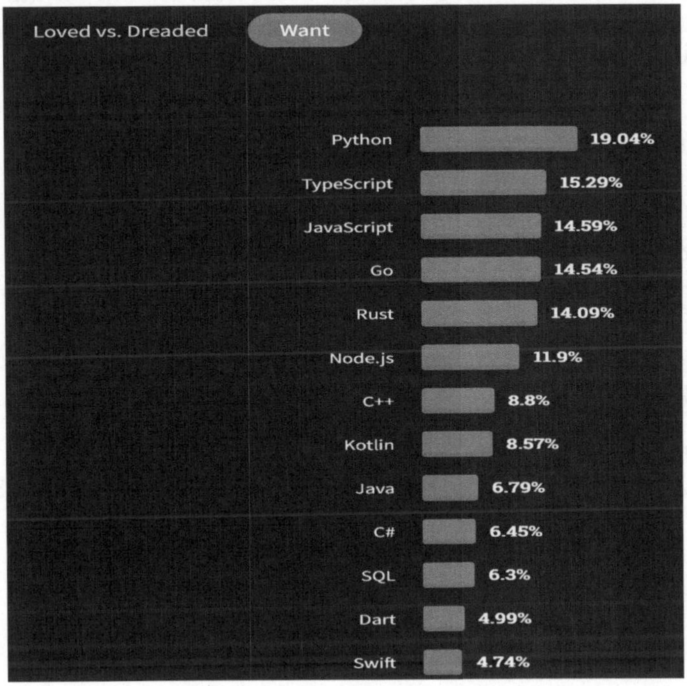

***Figure 1.7**: Most wanted languages by StackOverflow insights*

Moreover, another metric we would love to follow is the number of packages written in Go. This number of packages written in Go has already passed 1 Million packages (the data from July 2023). We link to an excellent website that collects data regarding open-source insights in the references at the end of the chapter. We highly recommend taking a look at it. If we compare the age and amount of packages written in Go versus other languages like Java, Python, or C#, Go leads right after JavaScript. That is unbelievable. The crazy amount of packages writing in Go came from the strong Golang community.

Conclusion

In this chapter, we took a short trip around microservices. We observed its history and what were the trends (Agile, cloud computing, Docker, DevOps) that led microservices to be so popular nowadays. We learned about the alternatives for microservices such as SOA, Monolith, and serverless. There are other alternatives in the market, but these are the most popular ones. We compared microservices' pros and cons and other architectures' pros and cons.

In the next chapter, we will talk about the usability of Golang. We will discuss the community and detail why we think and why the community thinks Go has become so popular in recent years. We will cover the ecosystem around Go and deep dive into why this language was invented in the first place. And what is the history from there until today? Finally, we will discuss the pros and cons of using Go.

References

- https://deps.dev/
- https://insights.stackoverflow.com/survey/2021?_ga=2.236209345.190202062.1628102352-126161871.1625855113#most-loved-dreaded-and-wanted-language-want
- https://trends.google.com/trends/explore?date=all&q=microservices&hl=en-GB
- https://agilemanifesto.org/
- https://trends.google.com/trends/explore?date=all&q=docker&hl=en-GB

CHAPTER 2
Usability of Go

Introduction

In this chapter, we'll delve into the incredible world of Go. We'll delve into the fundamentals, examine the history, and understand why the inventors wanted to invent this language. What was the intention behind creating such language, and what was it aimed for?

To understand Go, we aim to understand its core principles, paradigms, purposes, and so on. By understanding them, we will have the power to see the whole picture while writing code in Go. Many inexperienced Go developers start to write in Go and get annoyed by the error-handling technique. If they clearly understand the core principles, they will realize why Go's current error-handling manner is the precise solution.

We'll elaborate on each one of the core principles, understand their intention, and profit from their advantages. Then, we will observe on top of the process of newcomers to the language, from their onboarding until they upload their code to production.

Then, we will explore the Golang ecosystem. The ecosystem is a giant creature composed of many communities and Gophers. Since Golang is an open source maintained by Google, the adoption to join the community is enormous.

There is no need for prior knowledge of Go. It is suggested to revisit this chapter after gaining more experience as a Go developer. Many of the points we'll cover here may resonate better with you. A quote from "*Effective Go*" – "*In other words, to write Go well, it's important to understand its properties and idioms.*"

Structure

In this chapter, we will discuss the following topics:

- Invention of Go
- Core Principles and Paradigms
- Simplicity and Minimalist Design Approach
- A Fast Language that is Suitable for the Cloud
- Maintainability of Go

- From Onboarding to Production
- Go's Ecosystem – The Communities and Beyond

Invention of Go

So how was this language started? It all begins with Google. In 2007, three folks from Google decided to create a new language. The language was designed by Ken Thompson, Rob Pike, and Robert Griesemer, each bringing distinct yet related backgrounds to the table. They were involved in significant technological inventions such as UTF-8, Unix, C programming language, and so on. The full name of the language is Golang, which is a combination of "*go*" + "*lang*," in which "*lang*" is a shortcut for language. Instead, they prefer to call it Go and not Golang to emphasize that the language intends to be simple and memorable. The word "Go" is a common English term that implies movement, progress, and efficiency, which aligns with the language's purpose of providing a simple and efficient approach to software development. Also, "Go" are the first two letters of Google.

After getting the green light from Google, they started developing the language. One of their core internal agreements is that they will only include programming principles they all agree on. Although this language was invented in 2007, it was influenced mainly by the C programming language, which was created in 1972, and not by newer languages like C++, Java, C#, and so forth. There are many similarities between Go and C programming languages. Indeed, some people refer to Go as the modern version of C.

They started writing the programming language in Go, C++, and Assembly.

By 2008, many people within Google wanted to join this project. Very fast, it gained positive momentum within Google.

In 2009, Go was publicly announced as an open-source project via GitHub, and developers from everywhere could and wanted to contribute to the language. Also, the Gopher mascot we mentioned in the previous chapter was presented in 2009. There is a link to the project in the references.

Note that many other repositories in the organization called Go are super relevant and part of the Golang ecosystem, which we will discuss later. The decision to open-source the language and make it accessible to the world has been pivotal to its current success.

In 2012, the first version of Go 1.0 was published with the most extensive guarantee for simplicity and efficiency, which we will talk about later on in this chapter. From there, two versions of Go are being released yearly, except in 2012. Version 1.5 was the most significant. In that version, the compiler toolchain has been converted to Go entirely. Another fundamental version is 1.18, where generics and fuzzy testing concepts were presented. The current version of Go, which we will follow for this book, is 1.20 (July 2023).

Core Principles and Paradigms

While designing the Go programming language, the inventors had a few principles they led. Until today all of these core principles are still implemented. We can see it in every release note of Go. We recommend looking at the Go release note every time a new version is released. These release notes are not long; reading and understanding them takes approximately an hour. Investing 2-3 hours each year to stay updated on the language's latest developments is valuable. The release notes are clear, straightforward, and easily understandable.

As observed in the previous chapter, this language is designed to be well-suited for deployment on cloud computing platforms, multi-core computers, handling large codebases, and more.

Before delving into the specifics of each principle, it's essential to mention the official Go documentation titled "*Effective Go*." We recommend reading it; it's lucidly explained and straightforward. Another resource we find valuable is the code review comment wiki from Go's official GitHub organization - we recommend perusing and utilizing it.

There are three core principles for Go:

- **Simplicity**: Go is designed to be straightforward and easy to understand, with a clean syntax that avoids unnecessary complexity. This makes it easier for developers to write, read, and maintain code.
- **Efficiency**: Go is known for its speed and performance. It compiles directly to machine code, making it as fast as languages like C or C++ but with the ease of a higher-level language.
- **Maintainability**: Go emphasizes clear, modular code structures and strong typing, which helps prevent errors and makes it easier to update and refactor code over time.

*** Disclaimer - These core principles are not officially declared in Go's official documentation. I choose them..*

Go Paradigms

The Go programming language paradigms are officially declared in the documentation, including:

- Imperative
- Concurrent programming
- Object-Oriented

Imperative

Here's a brief overview of imperative programming: Imperative programming is a software paradigm in which the code aims to solve a problem step by step, and each line is supposed to lead us to solve the problem. It focuses on **how** to solve the problem. Imperative programming contrasts with declarative programming, which focuses more on declaring **what** we want to get. Examples of declarative languages are HTML, SQL, CSS, and so on. Go is an imperative language. Capabilities that show that Go is an imperative programming language are statements, variables, loops, and so on.

Concurrent programming

Concurrent programming involves designing software to execute multiple tasks simultaneously, often leading to improved performance and responsiveness in applications that handle multiple operations. We'll discuss in detail later how we can use Go concurrency. This paradigm is one of the core reasons for creating this language. Go can be multithreaded, multi-processing, and asynchronous, critical factors of a concurrent programming language.

Object-Oriented

"*Yes and no. Although Go has types and methods and allows an object-oriented style of programming, there is no type hierarchy. The concept of "interface" in Go provides a different approach that we believe is easy to use and, in some ways, more general. There are also ways to embed types in other types to provide something analogous–but not identical–to subclassing. Moreover, methods in Go are more general than in C++ or Java: they can be defined for any sort of data, even built-in types such as plain, "unboxed" integers. They are not restricted to structs (classes).*

Also, the lack of a type hierarchy makes "objects" in Go feel much more lightweight than in languages such as C++ or Java."

This quote is taken from Golang FAQ. The quote explains the object-oriented concept in Go quite well. Of course, we will discuss more in detail about composition in Go, on structs, interface, and so on.

Supported OOP Principles in Go:

- **Encapsulation**: Go supports encapsulation through packages and structs. We can define methods on structs to associate behavior with data, similar to methods in traditional OOP.
- **Composition**: Instead of classical inheritance, Go uses composition to build complex types from simpler ones, using a concept called embedding.

Not Supported OOP Principles in Go:

- **Inheritance**: Go does not support inheritance in the traditional sense. There are no classes, so we cannot define class hierarchies. Go's approach is to use interfaces and composition instead.
- **Polymorphism**: While Go does not support polymorphism through inheritance, it does support a form of polymorphism through interfaces. A single interface

can be implemented by multiple types, and a function that takes an interface as an argument can accept any type that implements the interface.

Go Properties

Another two properties of language are dynamic or static and strong or weak. For Go, these properties are:

- Statically typed
- Strong typing

Statically typed

Once the variable type is set in Go, we can't change it in runtime. We can't declare a variable without declaring its type. Note that we can do something like this:

```
x := 5
```

In that scenario, we don't explicitly declare the type, but Go uses "*type inference*" to decide the variable type. The inference does not always work until we use the `:=` operator.

In that use case, the inference type is int, of course.

Strong typing

What differentiates a "*strong*" programming language from a "*weak*" one is that we can do certain operations on variable types. Let's take this example:

```
myString := "name" + 2
```

This line will cause a compile error because we can't add an integer to a string.

Simplicity and Minimalist Design Approach

Numerous programming languages are currently widely used. A prevailing trend among many of these languages is that they have become similar with each new release. This similarity is characterized by a growing similarity in their capabilities and features.

Initially, each programming language was created with specific purposes in mind, and they had a limited set of capabilities and features. However, many enhancements occur with every subsequent version release of these languages. These updates include bug fixes, improvements, new features, extensions to core libraries, new libraries, new concepts, and so on.

Most programming languages adopt a "*more is better*" approach, continuously expanding their capabilities, features, and libraries, enabling them to handle various tasks.

Nevertheless, it is essential to note that this may not be the case for Go, as it deviates from this pattern of constant expansion.

Upon examining the release notes of Go, it becomes evident that most updates primarily focus on compilation enhancements, performance improvements, and accuracy refinements. While there are certainly some introductions of new features and capabilities (a significant example is generics), they don't make up the bulk of the changes. This emphasis on simplicity is what Go is aiming for. They want to keep Go **boring**.

An example of Go's simplicity and minimalism is the number of keywords in the language. Here is a graph showing the number of keywords.

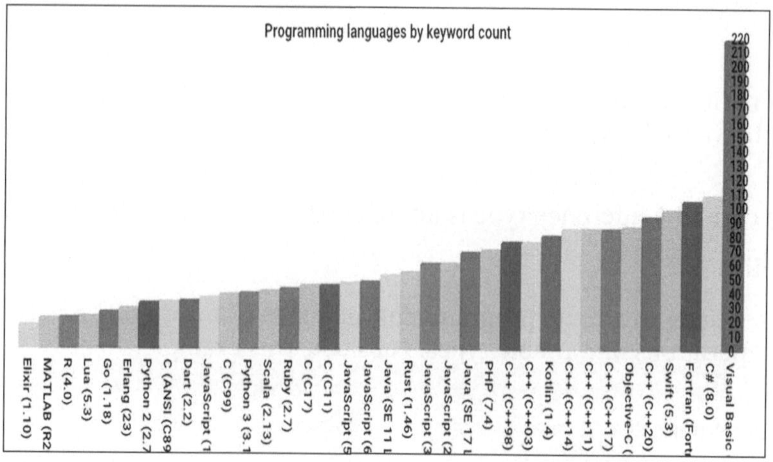

Figure 2.1: *Programming language by keyword count*

If a programming language has many keywords, it doesn't necessarily mean it's a bad language. Conversely, a language with a low number of keywords doesn't automatically indicate that it's a good programming language. The quality and effectiveness of a programming language depend on many factors beyond just the count of keywords it have.

But it is sure to say that it is easier to remember and use fewer keywords. We can see that Go is one of the languages with the lowest keywords.

Hidden complexity

There are many concepts within the language, and a lot of effort was put into them to create a powerful programming language on the one hand and a simple language on the other.

The concurrency approach is an excellent example of hidden complexity. We will talk in detail regarding the concurrency approach later in this chapter. It only requires three keystrokes to concurrency – **'g,' 'o'**, ' ' - that is amazing.

Another example of extreme simplicity is access modifiers. There are two scenarios. The function/variable/const can be private or public. To make something public in Go, we just need to do two things:

- It needs to be declared in the highest scope.
- It needs to be capitalized.

That's it; no need for extra keywords.

A few other simple things in Go:

- Garbage collection
- Consts
- Interfaces
- Packages

All of these examples have huge complexity behind the senses.

To summarize this section, Go doesn't compete in features. "As *for Go 1.0, the language is fixed.*"

A Fast Language Suitable for the Cloud

"*Go is fast and fun and productive.*" - Ken Thompson.

This was one of the core reasons why this language was invented: to provide fast language that can run concurrently on the cloud.

We will elaborate on three things that make Go so fast:

- Fast compiling
- Bearing a resemblance to C
- Concurrency approach

Fast Compiling

Rather than Go's intention to be fast in runtime, it also has a high intent to compile very fast, which is similar to the state of mind of the Agile methodology, where the release rate is significantly higher.

So what makes it compile so fast? And the binary to be so lean? Here are the reasons:

- Avoiding cyclic dependency
- Compilation design

- Unused imports and usages
- Go simplicity

Avoiding Cyclic Dependency

If we ever try to import packages in a cyclic fashion, we will encounter a complication error. Go can't compile if there are some cyclic dependencies. All the dependencies can be presented as a DAG (aka for Directed Acyclic Graph). Due to this package structure, each package can be compiled if all the packages in the tree are compiled before the package node.

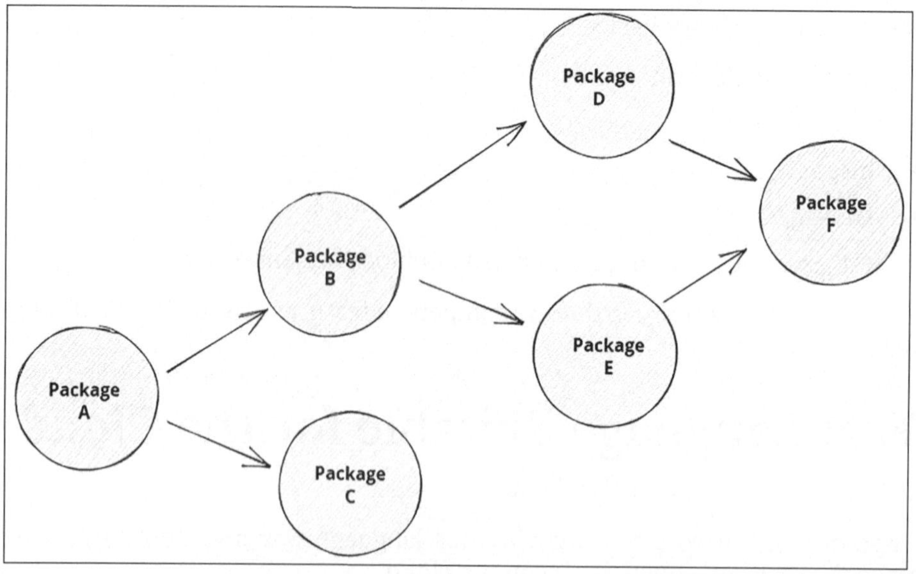

Figure 2.2: *Package dependencies DAG*

In this example, packages A and B were already compiled, and we can compile C, D, and E concurrently.

Compilation Design

A quote from Golang FAQ answering the question: "Why did you create a new language?"

"Finally, working with Go is intended to be fast: it should take at most a few seconds to build a large executable on a single computer. Meeting these goals required addressing a number of linguistic issues: an expressive but lightweight type system; concurrency and garbage collection; rigid dependency specification; and so on. These cannot be addressed well by libraries or tools; a new language was called for."

As we can see, one of the main reasons for creating Go was to develop a fast language that is easy to work with. This state of mind is and has always been in the minds of the Go team.

Unused imports and usages

In Go, we can't import a package that is not in use, and also, we can't declare a variable that is not in use. Both scenarios will lead us to get a compile error. Go will compile only the necessary dependencies, which leads to precise compilation and not compiling unused dependencies.

Go Simplicity

As previously mentioned, Go is a language known for its simplicity. The fact that it consists of only around 25 keywords makes the compilation process much more straightforward. This simplicity significantly pays off in terms of compilation time.

Bearing a Resemblance to C

Some individuals might characterize Go as a modern version of C. While many other languages typically use classes and inheritance, Go takes a different approach by utilizing structs and interfaces with composition. Go inherits various elements from both C and C++, such as data structures, pointers, the ability to pass by reference or value, and more.

C and C++ are renowned for their speed, and Go aims to achieve a similar level of performance. However, it also strives to be a modern and user-friendly language, making it easier to write code with enhanced productivity.

Concurrency Approach

Concurrency is a top priority in Go. Concurrent programming in Go is made simple and efficient through goroutines and channels. Goroutines are lightweight threads managed by the Go runtime, allowing multiple tasks to run independently. Channels are a way for goroutines to communicate with each other, enabling safe and synchronized data exchange, leading to faster and more scalable applications.

Goroutines and channels are first-class citizens. Concurrency is one of the core concepts that Go aims to establish and do well. We will take a short journey into Go's unique concurrency approach.

Go is a multi-threaded language. However, Go is different from other languages because, as a developer, we don't have direct access to the thread. That is implemented with the thought that threads are an asset of the OS. In Go, we should not care about threads. Of course, there are things to worry about, like access from different Goroutines to the same object (`sync` core library should help to tackle this concern through locks, unique objects, and so on).

Another concern is Goroutine's leak. Both of these concerns we will tackle in the following chapters.

So, what is Goroutine? The Go team wrapped the traditional thread through goroutines. They are highly cost-effective regarding resource usage and initialization.

Regarding memory footprint, initializing the Goroutine stack takes 2 KB, and the default thread stack is 8 KB. This is 4X more lightweight! The direct effect for Goroutines to be memory lightweight is that allocating and deallocating them is much faster than threads.

Goroutines are revolutionary, managed entirely by the Go runtime rather than the OS. They have accessible communication between themselves, lightweight memory, fast initialization, and are not hardware-dependent.

To explain how Goroutines works, let's talk about Go Scheduler. It is a component within the runtime of Go that has direct access to the kernel and is responsible for managing every Goroutine we execute.

Goroutines are scheduled on the thread themselves, and the Scheduler is responsible for allocating them on the thread.

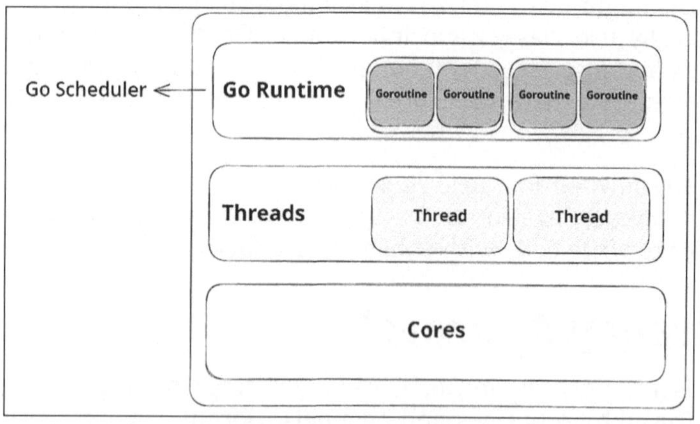

Figure 2.3: *Go scheduler*

In this figure, we can see the system's cores. The OS scheduler manages a layer of thread; above it, we can see our Go program that executes the Goroutines thread, and the Go Scheduler manages all of that.

Let's observe single-core system behavior.

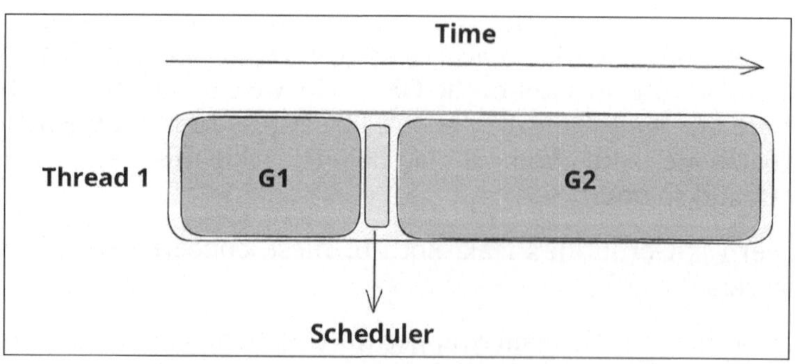

Figure 2.4: *Single-core OS allocating a goroutine*

This figure shows a single-core OS that executes some Goroutines called G1. Then another Goroutine is executed at the end, called G2.

But what happens when we have multi-cores? When a program starts in Go, the scheduler will initial a thread; if some goroutines are executed and the previous goroutines were not done, it allocates more threads until the maximum number of threads is reached. The maximum number of threads in a configuration is Go, which is set as an environment variable called **GOMAXPROCS**. The default and recommended value by a benchmark done by the Go team is the number of cores. For example, if a machine has 8 cores, the value of **GOMAXPROCS** is 8, and the scheduler won't schedule more than 8 threads. We can configure the environment variable, but this isn't recommended.

How does the scheduler work when more goroutines need to be executed rather than available threads?

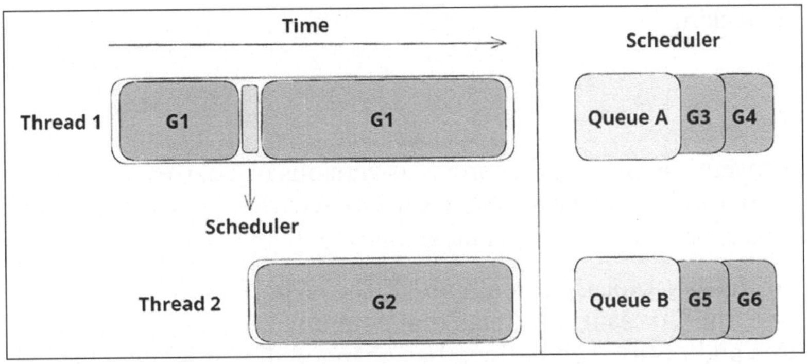

Figure 2.5: *Multiple threads with queues managed by the scheduler*

There is a dedicated queue for each thread that knows the next goroutines that are supposed to be scheduled on this thread. A new queue is created for each new thread being allocated. Each goroutine is allocated while running on some thread and directly goes to the same thread's queue. To prevent an intense load on a single queue, the scheduler performs work, stealing between threads and balances the work between them.

This was an explanation in a nutshell of the Go scheduler. There are many other things that the scheduler is considering, like system locks, code locks, communication between threads, allocating of threads, idle threads, and so on.

Maintainability of Go

Several reasons are why Go is easy to maintain:

- Compatibility
- Go simplicity
- Error handling

Compatibility

"It is intended that programs written to the Go 1 specification will continue to compile and run correctly, unchanged, over the lifetime of that specification. At some indefinite point, a Go 2 specification may arise, but until that time, Go programs that work today should continue to work even as future "point" releases of Go 1 arise (Go 1.1, Go 1.2, etc.)."

It is a quote from the documentation of Go when the first version of Go was released. There is an attachment to this documentation in the references. Note that later in the documents, they set expectations and write that things can go wrong, like bugs, security issues, structs literals, and more.

When every version of Go is released, there is an intention for backward and forward compatibility. According to Russ Cox from GopherCon 2022, the Go team uses two main approaches to keep it compatible:

- API Checking
- Testing

API Checking

In order to prevent the breakage of previous versions of Go, we can't remove exported symbols, API methods, packages, and so on. Otherwise, the program will fail. Go can't remove libraries, structs, methods, and so on.

The Go team uses a tool that contains all the exported API signatures for all Go versions. Then, the Go team runs tests that compare the package API to the exported API signatures and notify if something has changed. If something changes, they take action to either prevent it or at least minimize its impact.

Testing

A colossal advantage that Google maintains in Go is that it can be tested within Google. The development version of Go is being tested against all of Google's internal Go program tests. After all these tests pass, the Go development branch is used in the Google production environment and toolchain.

With every release of Go, they note if something got broken in the new version. Go also provides a powerful tool called `GODEBUG` that helps us upgrade our version and verify that our program doesn't panic.

Go Simplicity

As we have seen before, one of Go's main goals is simplicity. This simplicity pays off when we examine the program's maintainability. One significant advantage of the Go team is that they make all the rules. In the previous chapter, we talked about "*Effective Go*," which has all the conventions, best practices, and documentation for how to do things. Unlike some other languages where conventions come from different places, in Go, the Go team decides everything.

Error Handling

Go is different from other languages. In many other languages, we are expecting to see a **`try-catch-finally`** idiom.

This is not the case with Go. In Go, we will explicitly create an error and return it as a variable. Here is a quote from Go FAQ.

"We believe that coupling exceptions to a control structure, as in the `try-catch-finally` idiom, results in convoluted code. It also tends to encourage programmers to label too many ordinary errors, such as failing to open a file, as exceptional."

Sometimes it can be frustrating to see code like this:

```
if err != nil {
        return err
}
```

However, if we understand its motive, we can accept it. Additionally, to Go FAQ, the error handling in Go gives us a way to tell a story. Instead of just returning the error, we can add context to it and, by that, create the story of the error, for instance:

```
If err != nil {
        return fmt.Errorf("connecting to DB: %w", err)
}
```

Now we have the context that this error happened while trying to connect to the DB. It was just one example to understand the hidden power of error handling in Go.

From Onboarding to Production

A programming language doesn't consist only of language components like compiler, syntax, and so on. It also consists of several tools crucial to the toolchain, like a package manager, documentation, formatter, linter, test tools, and so on.

Go aims to give the Go developer a holistic experience by providing the tools in the toolchain. There are three reasons why the Go team wants to create the toolchain.

One is that they don't need to depend on anonymous contributors to create a tool. The second and more important reason is that the Go team knows the best way to build such a tool. The third reason is to achieve standardization.

We don't want to have two formatters that do very similar things but operate differently, and we can see these patterns in other languages. The formatter is just one example of standardization. It can be a linter, tests, time package, and so on.

What are the steps for the newcomer to the language until they deploy it to production?

1. Getting Started
2. Plan
3. Package Management
4. Writing code
5. Troubleshoot
6. Test
7. Security
8. Build
9. Others

1. **Getting Started**

A newcomer to the language doesn't know how the language syntax looks alike. The Go team created a playground, so developers who read about the language can already be engaged and play with it. All the documentation and playground exist in **`go.dev`**.

2. **Plan**

The newcomer fell in love with the language. Now, they want to start a project. But before jumping into the code, we want to plan. We want to understand how the project is going to look. To do so, we must understand and explore the packages we aim to use. There is a single artifact manager for all Go packages, and this manager, not surprisingly, exists in **`go.dev`**, specifically in **`pkg.go.dev`**.

3. **Package management**

To interact with various tools from the Go toolchain, we need to have the Go CLI; that's it. In the Go CLI, various tools help us to start the project. We finished planning our project, and now we want to start. We will run the following command to initial a project:

```
go mod init github.com/nirsht/microservices-with-go
```

If we want to install any package, we can run:

```
go install github.com/nirsht/myawesomepackage
```

There are a variety of tools that help us manage packages like **`go mod tidy`**, **`go vet`**, and so on. These commands are powerful and allow us to manage the packages.

4. **Writing code**

Once the project is set up and all the desired packages are incorporated, we can start writing code. We might opt for an integrated development environment (IDE) such as Visual Studio Code, Vim, or GoLand (developed by JetBrains) for efficient code composition. These IDEs, among others, rely on the Language Server Protocol (LSP) for their functionality.

Great definition of LSP by Microsoft:

"The language server protocol (LSP) is the product of standardizing the messages exchanged between a development tool and a language server process. Using language servers or demons is not a new or novel idea. Editors like Vim and Emacs have been doing this for some time to provide semantic auto-completion support"

For many programming languages, the LSP is not provided by the same author of the language. In Go, this is not the case. The LSP in Go is **`gopls`** and is maintained by the Go team. Moreover, the Go team also provides an extension for VScode called **`vscode-go`**.

5. **Troubleshoot**

Similar to all software engineers, our code sometimes functions flawlessly. Our efforts involve reading code, debugging, and troubleshooting annoying bugs. The Go team acknowledges this. They developed a tool intended to assist developers in debugging and troubleshooting. For instance, they offer the official Go debugger - **`gdb`**. Additionally, the Go team has developed an excellent profiler known as **`pprof`**, which enables the visualization and analysis of profiling data.

6. **Test**

Any software engineer who respects himself will add tests. This is an industry standard for creating maintainability of our system. Go also provides us with a tool to perform tests efficiently. No external library is needed, just the Go CLI. While running:

```
go test .
```

It will iterate over all the files and indicate the ones that have a postfix of **`_test`**, and then it will run all the functions with a prefix of **`Test`**.

The Go team provides several configurations within the **`go test`** command. My favorite is the option for testing race conditions through the Go CLI by running:

```
go test -race
```

From Go 1.18, fuzzy tests are available.

"Fuzzing is a type of automated testing which continuously manipulates inputs to a program to find bugs."

Fuzzy tests are a handy and powerful tool to verify that our program won't panic when we get wrong inputs.

7. **Security**

Now, we want to release our code for production. But there is a problem. We need to check that there are no security vulnerabilities in our package's dependencies.

Since Go 1.18, we can run a command to check all our vulnerabilities - **`govulncheck`**. Govulncheck is powered by the Go vulnerability database that is maintained by the Go team.

8. **Build**

The only thing remaining is to package our code. Go has a compiler that is responsible for compiling our code to the desired binary architect and OS. These can be configured easily by environment variables - **GOARCH** for architect and **GOOS** for OS.

The build command is built-in within the Go CLI, and we can use it by running:

```
go build main.go
```

9. **Others**

We have only covered a few tools of the Go toolchain on this journey. For keeping things consistent, Go centralizes several things like linting (checking code for errors, and more) and formatting (making code look neat, which is vital in Go). We believe the Go team has chosen suitable packages to include in the language, like the "time" package for handling time-related tasks.

Go's Ecosystem – The Communities and Beyond

Most of the programming languages today are OSS (aka Open-Source Software). Go is one of them, and it is OSS driven from its first days.

Nowadays, many people are thrilled and keen to contribute to Go or the many other projects in the Go development toolchain. Go is one of the most popular programming languages in terms of the number of packages (as we saw in the previous chapter).

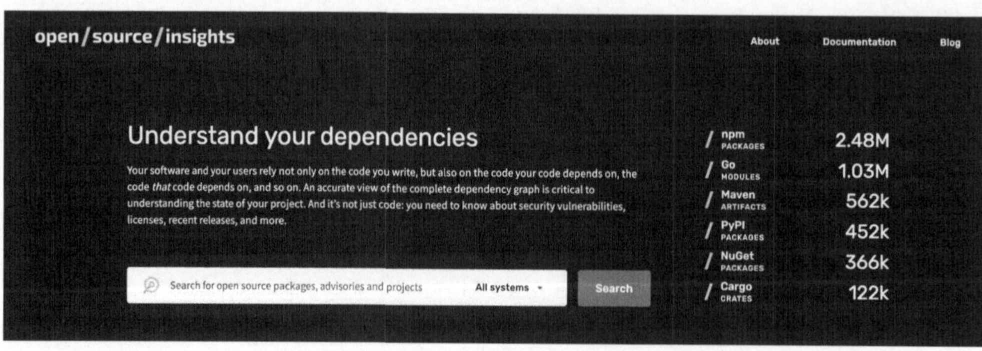

Figure 2.6: *The number of packages for leading OSS programming languages*

To improve one's skillset, knowledge, and personal performance in programming languages, it is essential to be involved in the ecosystem somehow. This can be by contributing to OSS projects, joining a community, or attending online or physical meetups. You can also join the Slack or Discord community.

A great website to view most of these opportunities is **gophersource**.

Conclusion

In this chapter, we learned the concepts that compose Go. Throughout Google's history, we saw the motivation and reason for creating this new language–simplicity, speed, maintainability, seamless onboarding, and so on.

Knowing all that stuff will give us the context that some things look like they look in Golang. The error handling in Go is a great example. Many newcomers to Go are struggling to understand why `try-catch-finally` doesn't exist. But, after a while, they understand why. The same goes for inheritance; many newcomers are initially surprised that inheritance doesn't exist, but after a while, they understand why composition is the precise choice for Go.

In the next chapter, we will explore the syntax and basics of Go. After we cover all the basics, we will approach more advanced topics.

We will discuss the simplicity concepts discussed in this chapter in more detail. Furthermore, we will delve into the implementation of concurrency and address the challenges that arise when employing concurrency in Go. Our discussions will encompass various topics, including composition, encapsulation, polymorphism, and more. Stay tuned!

References

- https://github.com/golang/go
- https://github.com/golang
- https://go.dev/doc/effective_go
- https://github.com/golang/go/wiki/CodeReviewComments
- https://go.dev/doc/faq#Is_Go_an_object-oriented_language
- https://github.com/e3b0c442/keywords
- https://go.dev/talks/2015/simplicity-is-complicated.slide
- https://go.dev/doc/go1compat
- https://www.youtube.com/watch?v=v24wrd3RwGo
- https://go.dev/play/
- https://github.com/golang/tools/tree/master/gopls
- https://go.dev/doc/gdb
- https://github.com/google/pprof
- https://go.dev/security/fuzz/
- https://gophersource.com/
- https://learn.microsoft.com/en-us/visualstudio/extensibility/language-server-protocol?view=vs-2022

CHAPTER 3
Go Essentials

Introduction

This chapter will delve into the fundamental aspects of Go, including its basic syntax, patterns, conventions, styles, and everything essential for becoming proficient in Go development. It will give newcomers and less experienced Go developers the minimum required knowledge to read this book.

This chapter will provide various code examples. All the code examples are available on the GitHub repository of this book. While reading this chapter, you are welcome to stop reading, practice code examples, or delve into a specific topic. If you decided to code while reading this chapter, it is recommended to code using Go Playground or VSCode (Visual Studio Code). But, use any IDE you find most suitable for you. There is no correct answer. We won't cover installation/environment setup instructions, which you are welcome to see in Go's official documentation - Effective Go.

Another thing worth mentioning here is that you already know how to program in another programming language. Based on this assumption, we won't cover programming concepts. We will cover those concepts' syntax, conventions, best practices, and semantics in Go.

This chapter serves as a concise overview of the Go programming language, designed to provide a quick and insightful introduction. It equips you with the foundational knowledge needed to derive value from the rest of the book.

Structure

In this chapter, we will discuss the following topics:

- Basic Overview of Golang
- Packaging – Accessing Between Packages
- Project Structure
- Structs
- Composition
- Interfaces

Basic Overview of Golang

Let's start exploring the basic syntax of Go!

Any programming language has a wide variety of syntax, keywords, libraries, and so on. We won't aim to cover them all. For that, you are welcome to read the Go documentation.

We will concentrate on the essentials so you can proceed with this book without going to external sources.

Regarding all the conventions and styles of Go, we recommend you read the Uber guide to styles and conventions in Go, which is very useful and easy to read. It is attached in the references. We aim to provide Go's most essential and basic styles and conventions.

Hello World

We will start with the most basic code example - a "Hello World" program example in Golang.

```
package main


import "fmt"


func main() {
        fmt.Println("Hello World!")
}
```

The command we used to run the program is:

```
go run Chapter-4/Hello-World/main.go
```

The first line:

```
package main
```

In Go, we use the saved keyword **`package`** and then use the package's name; in this case, the package name is **`main`**. The entry point package must be **`main`** to start a Go program.

After declaring the package, we'll declare the imports using the keyword **`import`** and then declare the package we want to import. In this example, the package name we use is **`fmt`**.

We can declare several packages in the same way:

```
import (
        "fmt"
        "os"
)
```

After declaring the package and the imports, we can declare types, consts, methods, and functions. In the example, we declared a function called **main,** the program's entry point in the **main** package.

We declared a function by using the keyword **func**, then declaring the function name, the parameters, "**{**" to open scope and "**}**" to close scope.

The **main()** function plays a crucial role as the entry point of a Go program, where execution begins. It is not a normal function; it is the running point to initiate the program's processes, making it essential for any Go application.

The last line:

```
fmt.Println("Hello World!")
```

This line functionality is to print the string - **Hello World!.** We used the function **Println**, which is a function inside the package **fmt**.

Another essential and saved function (rather than **main**) is **init()**. This will run at the program's start; it is the only function that runs before **main()**.

Variables

We have three ways to declare a variable in Go.

The first way is as follows:

```
var emptyMessage string
```

Here, we declare the keyword **var**, then the variable name - **emptyMessage**. In the example, the variable is of type string.

There is also an option to give a value to that variable while declaring it:

```
var message string = "This is a message"
```

Note that if we don't give it an initial value like in the first example, it will give it a default value. There is a different value for each primitive data type, nil for a pointer, and empty struct values for structs. We will elaborate on the default values of primitive data types later in this chapter.

The second way to declare a variable is to let the Go compiler infer the variable type by itself.

```
var inferredMessage = "This is an inferred message"
```

In that example, we didn't have to declare the **string**. The Go compiler inferred it from the syntax.

The third way to declare a variable in Go is by using **:=.**

```
alsoInferredMessage := "This is also an inferred message"
```

Here, we didn't have to declare the keyword **var** or **string,** just "**:=**".

In Go, variables can't change their type in runtime because Go is a static programming language, as we saw in *Chapter 2, Usability of Go.*

The convention for variables, functions, maps, structs, and everything we declare in Go is camelCase unless we want them to be public, in which case they will be PascalCase. We will discuss access modifiers in this chapter.

Primitive Data Types

Let's have a look at this code block:

```
package main

import "fmt"

func main() {
	message := "This is a message"
	fmt.Println(message)

	var zero int
	fmt.Println(zero)

	number := 42
	fmt.Println(number)

	var pi float64 = 3.14
	fmt.Println(pi)

	var booleanVar bool
	fmt.Println(booleanVar)

	trueBooleanVar := true
	fmt.Println(trueBooleanVar)
}
```

There are four primitive data types in Go - **`string`, `boolean`, `float32` (also `float64`),** and **`int`** (also **`int8`**, **`int 16`**, **`int32`**, **`int64`**, **`uint`**, **`unit8`**, **`unit16`**, **`unit32`**, **`unit64`**).

- **`string`** is for text. The default value is an empty text "".
- **`int`** is for a whole number. The default value is **`0`**.
- **`float32`** is for a floating point number. The default value is **`0`**.
- **`bool`** is for **`true`** or **`false`**. The default value is **`false`**.

As we saw before, we can declare a variable without declaring the type, but the type will be inferred. Go will choose the most convenient type. For instance, if we want the variable to be **int8** and not **int,** we must declare it. Otherwise, the Go compiler will choose an **int**.

Comments

There are two types of comments:

- single-line
- multiline

Here is a single-line example:

```
func main() {
        // This is simple comment
}
```

Here is a multiline example:

```
/*
        This is a multi-line comment
*/
fmt.Println("Hello World!")
```

For single-line comments, use **//** and for multiline, start with **/*** and end with ***/**.

Operators

Let's put here an example for all the operators in Go. The operators in Go are very similar to any other programming language.

```
package main


func main() {
        // Arithmetic Operators
        x := 5 + 5 // 10
        x = 5 - 5  // 0
        x = 5 * 5  // 25
        x = 5 / 5  // 1
        x = 5 % 5  // 0
        x++        // 6
        x--        // 5
```

```
    // Comparison Operators
    y := 5 == 5 // true
    y = 5 != 5  // false
    y = 5 > 5   // false
    y = 5 < 5   // false
    y = 5 >= 5  // true
    y = 5 <= 5  // true

    // Logical Operators
    a := true && true // true
    a = true && false // false
    a = true || true  // true
    a = true || false // true
    a = !true         // false
    a = !false        // true

    // Bitwise Operators
    b := 5 & 5 // 5
    b = 5 | 5  // 5
    b = 5 ^ 5  // 0
    b = 5 << 5 // 160
    b = 5 >> 5 // 0

    // Assignment Operators
    c := 5
    c += 5  // 10
    c -= 5  // 5
    c *= 5  // 25
    c /= 5  // 5
}
```

If statement

Like other languages, the keywords that exist are **if and else**. Also, their usage is exactly the same.

Loops

There are various ways to make loops in Go; all of them use the keywords **for**, and for break, use **break**, and to move to the next iteration, use **continue** -

```
func main() {

	// for loop with initialization, condition, and post
	for i := 0; i < 5; i++ {
		println(i)
	}

	// for loop with single condition, act as a "while"
	i := 0
	for i < 5 {
		println(i)
		i++
	}

	// for loop with no condition, act as a "while"
	i = 0
	for {
		println(i)
		i++
		if i >= 5 {
			break
		}
	}

	// for loop with continue
	for i := 0; i < 5; i++ {
		if i%2 == 0 {
			continue
		}
		println(i)
	}
```

```
        // for loop with range
        s := []int{1, 2, 3}
        for k, v := range s {
                println(k, v)
        }
}
```

Note that there isn't **while** keyword in Go. For a while loop, we just use **for** (with or without a condition).

The last example of a for loop with range is unique to Go. The **range** keyword lets us iterate on iterable types such as array, slice, and map.

Arrays

There are two ways to declare an array in Go:

```
func main() {
        // declare an array of 5 integers
        var a = [5]int{1, 2, 3, 4, 5}
        // declare an array with inferred length
        var b = [...]int{1, 2, 3}
}
```

In the first example (**var a = [5]int{1, 2, 3, 4, 5}**), the length was set to 5. In the second example (**var b = [...]int{1, 2, 3}**), the length was inferred. Of course, we can declare an array without using the keyword **var** and just using **:=**.

Arrays in Go can only store the same type, and the length of arrays is immutable.

Slices

Slices are very similar data type to an array, but slices are much more flexible. The length of the slice can change in the runtime. Slices are one of Go's main strengths. Here is how we declare a slice in Go:

```
mySlice := []string{"nir", "david"}
```

The declaration is almost the same syntax as arrays, but we don't need to declare the size (or infer it by "..."). Another way to declare a slice in Go is by using the **make** keyword.

```
mySlice := make([]type, length, capacity)
```

The **length** is the number of elements the slice contains, whereas the **capacity** is the number of elements in the backing array, counting from the first element in the slice.

The **capacity** will always be bigger than the **length**.

Two functions that help us to determine arrays, slice length, and capacity are **len** (for measuring length) and **cap** (for measuring capacity).

```
slice := make([]int, 2, 5)
fmt.Println(slice) // [0 0]
fmt.Println(len(slice)) // 2
fmt.Println(cap(slice)) // 5
```

A convenient operation we can do is split a slice/array into portions. Here is an example of doing so.

```
myArray := [5]int{1, 2, 3, 4, 5}
slice = myArray[1:4] // from the 1st index to the 4th index (not included)
fmt.Println(mySlice) // [2 3 4]
```

Functions

In Go, a function can return several parameters with different data types:

```
func myFunction(amount int, prefix string) string {
	return fmt.Sprintf("%s: %d", prefix, amount)
} // Input: 5, "nir" | Output: "nir: 5"


func multipleReturns(prefix string, amount int) (string, int) {
	amount++
	return fmt.Sprintf("%s: %d", prefix, amount), amount
} // Input: "nir", 5 | Output: "nir: 6", 6


func namedReturnValues(prefix string, amount int) (result string,
newAmount int) {
	amount++
	result = fmt.Sprintf("%s: %d", prefix, amount)
	newAmount = amount
	return
} // Input: "nir", 5 | Output: "nir: 6", 6
```

In the first example (**myFunction**), we can see a simple function, using the **func** and **return** keywords. In the second example (**multipleReturns**), we see a function with multiple return values. In the third example (**namedReturnValues**), we see a function with multiple named return values (a single named return value is also valid).

An instrumental ability to Go regarding functions is to use **defer**. The **defer** keyword is a function. This function gets executed after the parent function finishes its functionality. Here are two examples:

```
func functionWithDefer() {
	defer fmt.Println("This will be printed last")
	fmt.Println("This will be printed first")
} // Output: This will be printed first
//         This will be printed last

func functionWithMultipleDefers() {
	defer func() {
		fmt.Println("This will be printed last")
	}()
	defer fmt.Println("This will be printed second")
	fmt.Println("This will be printed first")
}

// Output: This will be printed first
//         This will be printed second
//         This will be printed last
```

The examples are pretty straightforward and explain the purpose of the **"defer"** function.

In Go, functions are first-class citizens, which can be passed as arguments to other functions, returned from functions, and assigned to variables. This feature enables the creation of higher-order functions and facilitates functional programming patterns.

Maps

Maps in Go are used to store key-value data. The default value of the **map** in Go is **nil**. Maps hold references to an underlying hash table. Here is how we declare a map and some common actions on **map**:

```
fruitsPrices := map[string]int{
	"orange": 10,
	"apple":  20,
	"banana": 15,
```

```
}
fmt.Println(fruitsPrices) // Output: map[apple:20 banana:15 orange:10]

// Add a new key-value pair
fruitsPrices["mango"] = 25
fmt.Println(fruitsPrices) // Output: map[apple:20 banana:15 mango:25
orange:10]

// Delete a key-value pair
delete(fruitsPrices, "orange")
fmt.Println(fruitsPrices) // Output: map[apple:20 banana:15 mango:25]

// Get a value from a map
fmt.Println(fruitsPrices["apple"]) // Output: 20

// Get a value from a map that doesn't exist
fmt.Println(fruitsPrices["grapes"]) // Output: 0 (the default value for
int)

// Check if a key exists in a map
price, ok := fruitsPrices["grapes"]
fmt.Println(price, ok) // Output: 0 false

// Iterate over a map
for fruit, price := range fruitsPrices {
	fmt.Printf("%s: %d\n", fruit, price)
} // Output: apple: 20 banana: 15 mango: 25 (order may vary)

fmt.Println(len(fruitsPrices)) // Output: 3

// Create an empty map
emptyMap := make(map[string]int)
fmt.Println(emptyMap) // Output: map[]
```

Switch

Use the **switch** statement when selecting one of many code blocks. In Go, the keyword **break** is unnecessary; it breaks by **default** after every case. If you wish to go through the next switch case, use the **fallthrough** keyword. Here are typical examples:

```
func main() {
	printString("b") // b
	printString("a") // a b
}

func printString(str string) {
	switch str {
	case "a":
		println("a")
		fallthrough
	case "b":
		println("b")
	default:
		println("default")
	}
}
```

If none of the expressions matches, it will go to the **default** statement.

Consts

We can declare consts in the same scopes as variables using the `const` keyword. During runtime, constants cannot be altered or manipulated. The available types for consts are numbers, characters (runes), strings, or booleans. (For more information about runes, check Reference number 5). Here are examples that demonstrate consts in Go:

```
const str string = "const string"

const (
	_ = iota
	one
	two
	three
```

```
)

func main() {

        println(str)        // string
        str = "new string" // cannot assign to str, will fail in compilation

        println(one)   // 1
        println(two)   // 2
        println(three) // 3
}
```

First, declaring a const string is pretty straightforward. Note that we used the keyword **`string`** in the example, which isn't essential.

Second, the example of **`iota`**. The **`iota`** identifier represents integer-based constants in Go and is a convenient way to declare a sequence of constants while keeping the code readable. The initial value of **`iota`** is 0.

Other Language Specifications

In the next sections, we will cover different topics that weren't covered in the earlier section, such as bytes, error, channels, goroutines, generics, structs, interfaces, libraries, pointers, the empty interface, type conversion, and more. We can always check the Go language specification.

Packages

A package in Go is a way to divide a program into smaller parts. The Go compiler comes with several standard packages that are widely common and popular. Those packages include **`fmt, log, net, strconv, strings, sync, testing, os, math, errors`**, and so on.

We can explore all publicly available Go packages for use at https://pkg.go.dev/.

As mentioned in the Hello World introduction, we import a package using the **`import`** keyword at the beginning of our file. Additionally, we have the option to rename a package like this:

```
import (
        f "fmt"
        "math"
)
```

We renamed **fmt** to **f**. The naming convention in Go for packages is short and mainly single words like nouns. The only available character except for a-z and numbers we can use in the package name is **_**.

The naming in Go is critical for accessing or viewing things outside a package. It is determined by whether the first character of a variable is uppercase (the same goes for function, consts, struct, and more).

```
const myName = "jack" // not public


const MyName = "jack" // public
```

To work on a project, we need to initialize a new module. To do so, we need to run this line, for instance:

```
go mod init githubple.com/nir/mymodule
```

It will create a new file called **go.mod**, which includes the module name, the Go version, the entire package, and the versions we use in that module.

After we declare the modules we want to use, the **go.mod** file should look like this:

```
module github.com/OrangeAVA/Microservices-with-Go


go 1.21.0


require (
	github.com/gin-gonic/gin v1.9.0
)
```

To download the package, we should run:

```
go mod download
```

It will create/update a file called **go.sum**, which maintains the checksums of the dependencies used in the project. The **go.sum** file ensures that the project uses the exact same versions of dependencies in subsequent builds, enhancing the reproducibility and security of the build process. We don't need to change or edit this file, as it is auto-generated by the Go toolchain.

Occasionally, we might encounter **// indirect** following a package requirement. This occurs when we don't directly utilize the module in our project, but one of our dependencies relies on it.

A convenient command that helps us to include only the imports that we need is:

```
go mod tidy
```

This command removes all the dependencies that we don't use.

Project Structure

There are many practices regarding the project structure and many use cases. We will elaborate on the important ones. The more detailed file structure is in the references. Here is a tree of the Go project's standard and the crucial files and directories.

```
.
├── cmd
│   ├── cli
│   │   └── main.go
│   └── server
│       └── main.go
├── go.mod
├── go.sum
├── internal
│   └── handlers
│       ├── handler1.go
│       └── handler2.go
└── pkg
    └── api
        ├── api.go
        └── api_test.go
```

***Figure 3.1:** Minimal file structure in Go*

As we saw before, we must have **`go.mod`** and **`go.sum`** files to start a Go project. Rather than those files, three crucial directories are - **`cmd`**, **`internal`**, and **`pkg`**.

"`cmd`" directory - includes all the entry points of my code, and the directory name of each program should match the name of the binary.

"`pkg`" directory - needs to include all the code that is fine to share with other services. This should consist of a common code that can be useful for other services. Note that there is usually a single pkg directory for all the services when we work with a mono repo, and there isn't a pkg directory within each service.

"`internal`" directory - private packages used internally for the service.

Structs

Go's structs are typed collections of fields. The struct in Go is used to create records.

Here is how we declare a struct in Go:

```
type user struct {
        name  string
        email string
}
```

While declaring a struct, we can only declare the struct fields. Another way to create structs is through embedded structs:

```
type admin struct {
	user
	level string
}
```

Here, we embedded the user struct within the admin struct. To create a new instance of a struct, we need to declare it and include its parameters; if some parameter is missed, it will give it the parameter's default value.

```
u1 := user{
	name:  "john",
email: "john@gmail.com",
}
fmt.Printf("%+v\n", u1) // {name:john email:john@gmail.com}
```

There isn't a built-in constructor to create a struct in Go. The convention in Go for creating a struct is through a function, and the function should have a prefix of **new** or **New** if it is public, for instance:

```
func newUser(name string) user {
	return user{
		name:  name,
		email: fmt.Sprintf("%s@gmail.com", name),
	}
}


u2 := newUser("jack")
fmt.Printf("%+v\n", u2) // {name:jack email:jack@gmail.com}
```

We declared a function called **newUser**, which accepts only **name** and, from there, generates the email. We could use any functionality that we believe is the right one. Let's see an example of declaring an embedded struct:

```
a := admin{
	user: user{
		name:  "john",
		email: "john@gmail.com",
	},
```

```
    level: "super",
}
fmt.Printf("%+v\n", a) // {user:{name:john email:john@gmail.com} level:-
super}
```

To access/modify a value of a struct instance, we can do it like this:

```
u3 := newUser("amanda")
fmt.Printf("%+v\n", u3) // {name:amanda email:amanda@gmail.com}
fmt.Println(u3.name)    // amanda - we access the field name of the
struct user
u3.name = "ruth"  // we change the value of the field name of the struct
user
fmt.Printf("%+v\n", u3) // {name:ruth email:amanda@gmail.com}
```

Go supports methods defined on struct types. It means we declare a function on the same scope as the struct and assign it to it. Let's see an example:

```
func (u user) Print() {
    fmt.Printf("Name: %s, Email: %s\n", u.name, u.email)
}
```

We declared the **Print** method in the same scope as the **user** struct. Note that this example is a struct method as a value receiver. We can also define a method to a struct as a pointer receiver so the method can mutate the struct fields. For instance:

```
func (u *user) ChangeEmail(email string) {
    u.email = email
}
```

Composition

Composition lets us create complex things by combining simpler parts, making our code more modular and flexible. The inheritance feature doesn't exist in Go. Let's observe an example of composition:

```
type Animal struct {
    Sound string
}

func (a *Animal) Speak() {
    println(a.Sound)
}
```

```
type Cat struct {
	Animal // Embedding
}

type Dog struct {
	Animal // Embedding
}

func main() {
	cat := Cat{Animal{"Meow"}}
	cat.Speak() // Meow

	dog := Dog{Animal{"Woof"}}
	dog.Speak() // Woof
}
```

We implemented a struct called **`Animal`** with a **`Speak`** method. We also created two different structs called **`Cat`** and **`Dog`** that both embedded the **`Animal`** struct. By doing so, those structs inherit all the properties and methods of the **`Animal`** struct.

Interfaces

Interface in Go slightly differs from other languages. In Go, interfaces contain only method signatures and not fields. We can't create an interface instance in Go, but we can declare a variable assigned to some type that fulfills the interface method signatures. Let's take a look at the following example:

```
type Person struct {
	Name string
}

func (m Person) Print() {
	fmt.Println(m.Name)
}

type DogPerson struct {
	Name string
```

```
}

type PrintInterface interface {
	Print()
}

var PrintableObject PrintInterface = Person{}
var PrintableObject2 PrintInterface = DogPerson{} // This will throw an error in compile time
```

We declared an interface called **PrintInterface** with a **Print()** signature. When we declared **PrintableObject**, it was okay because the **Person** struct implemented the **Print** method. On the other hand, when we try to declare **PrintableObject2**, it causes a compilation error because the **DogPerson** struct doesn't satisfy the **PrintInterface** interface.

A vital and widely used interface in Go is the "empty interface". The "empty interface" is a type that specifies zero methods and looks like this - **interface{}**

```
var i interface{}
Or
var myName interface{}
```

The empty interface is unique because it can hold values of any type (every type implements at least 0 methods). Its primary usage is handling unknown situations, which we will encounter many times throughout the book.

Conclusion

We have addressed the foundational knowledge and syntax necessary for comprehending this book. We covered the basis of any programming language - variables, loops, operators, code style, arrays, maps, and comments. We also covered specific syntax related to Go, such as packages, structs, interfaces, and project structure. Feel free to explore the Go language specifications further through the references provided in this chapter.

In the upcoming chapters, we will dive into more advanced Go topics, although it's important to acknowledge that we will only cover a portion. If you are a newcomer to Go, you can continue your exploration of the Go language by yourself.

References

- https://github.com/uber-go/guide/blob/master/style.md
- https://go.dev/doc/effective_go#init

- https://go.dev/doc/install
- https://www.w3schools.com/go/go_variable_naming_rules.php
- https://www.educative.io/answers/what-is-the-rune-type-in-golang
- https://github.com/golang-standards/project-layout
- https://go.dev/ref/spec#Clear

CHAPTER 4
Embarking on the Go Journey

Introduction

This chapter delves further into the intricacies of coding in Go. Unlike the preceding chapter, all Go developers should read this chapter. Although we will still cover known topics in Go, we will discuss the connection between those topics and Microservices. We will cover design patterns that exist in Go.

Design patterns are a great way to solve common problems that happen to us as developers, regardless of which language we write in. Almost all the known design patterns are common to each language and look similar. There is an excellent website called `https://refactoring.guru/design-patterns`, where we can look at and explore design patterns. It is very convenient and has excellent examples demonstrating each design pattern in various popular programming languages; as you probably guessed, one is Golang.

While we won't cover general coding principles like SOLID, YAGNI, KISS, and DRY, it's important to mention Uncle Bob's Clean Code when discussing coding concepts. This book is essential for every developer, and Uncle Bob also has a more entertaining YouTube version of the book.

We will cover four crucial concepts in Go - generics, context, errors, and testing. If we master those things, we will make our code much more resilient, readable, and maintainable.

Structure

In this chapter, we will discuss the following topics:

- Functional Options Pattern
- Generics
- Understanding Context in Go
- Errors - Talking About Error Propagation

- Testing - Best Practices, Mocking, Fuzzy Tests
- Microservices Testing

Functional Options Pattern

The decision was made to focus specifically on this pattern and not on other design patterns for two reasons. The first reason is that this design pattern is relatively distinctive within the context of Go and is one of the most used design patterns we can think of (maybe Singleton or Adapter are more popular).

This pattern helps to construct `structs` cleanly and precisely. This is because Go does not support overloading (overloading creates a function in the same name but with a different signature). Also, there aren't optional parameters in functions in Go.

Those two facts (overloading and optional parameters not supported) can make our life of building a **`struct`** very hard. Building a structure can become a mess with many configurations (usually expressed as optional parameters). The functional options pattern lets us create a single struct constructor that receives the required parameters and a list of optional parameters. The steps to use this pattern are:

1. Create your desired **`struct.`**
2. Create a type which is the name of the start + postfix of `Option` (**`{structName} Options`**) that is equal to **- `func(*{structName})`**.
3. Create your constructor `New{structName}`, include the required parameters, and add **`options …{structNameOptions}`** and return **`*{structName}.`**
4. Create a custom function for each option. The convention is to start each one of those functions with a prefix of **`With`**.

Let's illustrate those steps; we created a struct of shopping client that looks like this:

```
type ShoppingClient struct {
	endpoint string
	apiKey   string
	userId   string

	shouldRetry bool
	timeout     time.Duration
}
```

The second step is to create the option type:

```
type ShoppingClientOption func(*ShoppingClient)
```

Now, we can make our constructor that should look like this:

```
func NewShoppingClient(endpoint string, options ...ShoppingClientOption)
*ShoppingClient {
	client := &ShoppingClient{
		endpoint: endpoint,
	}

	for _, option := range options {
		option(client)
	}

	return client
}
```

Note that if we don't give any option, the fields will get their default value, except **endpoint**, which is required field. All that is left is to create the option functions.

```
func WithApiKey(key string) ShoppingClientOption {
	return func(c *ShoppingClient) {
		c.apiKey = key
	}
}

func WithUserId(id string) ShoppingClientOption {
	return func(c *ShoppingClient) {
		c.userId = id
	}
}

func WithTimeout(timeout time.Duration) ShoppingClientOption {
	return func(c *ShoppingClient) {
		c.timeout = timeout
	}
}
```

```
func WithRetry(shouldRetry bool) ShoppingClientOption {
	return func(c *ShoppingClient) {
		c.shouldRetry = shouldRetry
	}
}
```

Let's demonstrate two usages of the pattern:

```
client := NewShoppingClient("https://api.shopping.com/v1",
	WithApiKey("my-api-key"),
	WithTimeout(10*time.Second),
)
fmt.Printf("%+v\n", client) // &{endpoint:https://api.shopping.com/v1
apiKey:my-api-key userId: shouldRetry:false timeout:10000000000}


clientV2 := NewShoppingClient("https://api.shopping.com/v2",
	WithRetry(true),
	WithUserId("my-user-id"),
)
fmt.Printf("%+v\n", clientV2) // &{endpoint:https://api.shopping.com/v2
apiKey: userId:my-user-id shouldRetry:true timeout:0}
```

In the examples, we created two clients with different configurations. We applied only the configuration needed in each example, which is this pattern's strength. Remember this important design pattern because it will become handy further in the book.

Generics

Generics is a new feature and was introduced in v1.18. Go have a support generics from version 1.18. Among the significant additions to the language, Generics stand out as a prominent concept.

Generics in programming let us write flexible and reusable code by handling different types of data in a more adaptable way.

This section will cover the essentials of generics in Go and the points where they differ from other languages. Generics exist for functions, structs, interfaces, and maps. Generic behavior in Go is similar to other languages, but some differences exist. We assume that the reader has a previous knowledge of Generics. By assuming that, we won't elaborate on the concept of Generics here.

A good explanation starts with the simplest example; here is a generic function:

```
func printIt[T any](item T) {
	fmt.Println(item)
}

printIt(1)       // 1
printIt("Hello") // Hello
```

By using [and] to declare the generic type of the function, which in this case is `any` and represented by **`T`**. The only thing that differs mainly from other languages with generics is `any` keyword. Each generic representation (in the preceding example, **`T`**) must implement an interface or constraints.

For constraints - there are two built-in constraints - **`any`** and **`comparable.`**

For interfaces - the Go team provided us with a convenient package called **`golang.org/x/exp/constraints`**, which gives us common constraints interfaces for generics.

1. **Any:** Anything, meaning each type, can fulfill this constraint.
2. **`Comparable`:** Pertains to any type, we can apply comparison operators such as == and **!=**. That map keys must be comparable.
3. **`Interfaces`**: we can create our custom interface as a constraint to our generic function; see the following example:

    ```
    type Number interface {
    	int | float64
    }

    func bigger[T Number, K any](a T, b T, prefix K) {
    	if a > b {
    		fmt.Println(prefix, a)
    		return
    	}
    	fmt.Println(prefix, b)
    }

    bigger(1, 2, "The bigger integer is:")   // The bigger integer is: 2
    bigger(3.0, 2.0, "The bigger float is:") // The bigger float is: 3
    ```

We declare a custom interface called `Number`, which includes two types using the pipe symbol **|**. The other examples are similar to the first example.

We can also apply generic to structs. It can be advantageous to build a flexible **struct** for many types. Let's take an example of a storage **struct** that can store an item and fetch that item.

```
type StorageInter[T any] interface {
	GetItem() T
	StoreItem(T)
}

type Storage[T any] struct {
	Item T
}

func (s *Storage[T]) GetItem() T {
	return s.Item
}

func (s *Storage[T]) StoreItem(item T) {
	s.Item = item
}
```

The preceding code snippet has complex logic compared to the one we discussed in the previous section. First, we declared a generic interface, which is possible in Go. Then, we declared a simple generic struct with a property called `Item` whose type is `T`, and the `T` constraint is any. Then, we implemented the **StorageInter** interface functions signature. To make sure the struct implements the interface, we declared the following line:

```
var _ StorageInter[int] = &Storage[int]{}
```

It is worth mentioning that this is a superb way in general (regardless of Generics) to make sure that a struct fulfills an interface (declare an empty variable - **"_"**). The usage of this function would look the same as any usage of struct in Go. The only difference is that we need to instantiate the type (**[int]**) because it is generics. To understand this in a better way, let us discuss the following code examples:

```
var intStorage StorageInter[int] = &Storage[int]{}
intStorage.StoreItem(789)
fmt.Println(intStorage.GetItem())

var stringStorage StorageInter[string] = &Storage[string]{}
```

```
stringStorage.StoreItem("This is a string")
fmt.Println(stringStorage.GetItem())
```

In the preceding two examples, we illustrate how to use a generic `struct` in Golang. In the first example, we apply the type of **`int`** to the **`struct`** `Storage`, and in the second example, we apply the type of **`string`** to the **`struct`** `Storage`. Because the signature of `StoreItem` function is **`StoreItem(item T)`**, we can pass int the first example and pass string in the second example.

Understanding Context in Go

In Golang, Context is one of the Core pillars that every Golang developer should know.

The Go team created a **`Context`** package, which helps us manage context. It's as simple as that. Behind the sense, context is a struct. We can only observe its interface - **`context.Context`** (from the **`context`** package), which looks like this:

```
type Context interface {
        Deadline() (deadline time.Time, ok bool)
        Done() <-chan struct{}
        Err() error
        Value(key any) any
}
```

An in-depth discussion of interface signatures is beyond the scope of this chapter. In simple words, for understanding, we can divide into three concepts:

1. **Manage key-value store**: In a second, we can save and retrieve values from context by keys. We can get values from context by a function in the **`context`** package - **`Value(key any) any`**.
2. **Handling concurrency**: In the next chapter, we'll explore concurrency. The context is an elementary tool that helps us leverage communication between goroutines.
3. **Managing tasks:** Using **`context`**, we can ensure that related tasks can gracefully stop when needed by passing values, cancellation signals, and deadlines (timeout).

To start using **`context`**, let's see how to create a **`context`** from nothing using the function **`context.Background()`**

```
ctx := context.Background()
```

We should avoid using this function if unnecessary and strive to use the parent **`context`**. We will see in a moment how to do it.

As we saw, one of the goals of context is to serve key-value stores. Let's examine an instance where we aim to include the API key within the context.

```
func main() {
	ctx := context.Background()
	childContext := context.WithValue(ctx, "apiKey", 123456)
	printAPIKey(childContext)
}

func printAPIKey(ctx context.Context) {
	apiKey := ctx.Value("apiKey")
	fmt.Println("API Key:", apiKey) // API Key: 123456
}
```

We used the function of **`context.WithValue`,** which gets the parent context and key value. Note that these functions get any type as a parameter (`any` is an alias to the empty interface - **`interface{}`**).

Context serves various purposes, such as task management, timeouts, environment variables, and more. To illustrate context usage, consider a scenario in task management where we must stop and gracefully terminate a task. The **`Context`** package provides a solution through the `WithCancel` function, generating a side function that cancels the context and adds an error. This allows us to gracefully terminate tasks using the `WithCancel` function, and we can retrieve an error using the **`Err()`** function. Let's look at an example of canceling a context for better understanding.

```
contextWithCancel, cancel := context.WithCancel(ctx)
cancel()
fmt.Println("What happened ?", contextWithCancel.Err()) // What happened
? context canceled
```

Another way to conceal context is by using timeout. As an illustration, we know tasks must adhere to a 30-second timeout, or it could affect our DB. Let's see an example of doing it while using the function **`context.WithTimeout(parent Context, timeout time.Duration) (Context, CancelFunc)`.**

```
contextWithTimeout, _ := context.WithTimeout(ctx, 30*time.Second)
fmt.Println("What happened ?", contextWithTimeout.Err()) // What hap-
pened ? <nil>
time.Sleep(35 * time.Second)
fmt.Println("What happened ?", contextWithTimeout.Err()) // What hap-
pened ? context deadline exceeded
```

Another useful function is a **`WithDeadline`.** This function lets us define a specific time when the context is done. Note that the function **`WithTimeout`** uses the **`WithDeadline`** function behind the senses.

```
func WithTimeout(parent Context, timeout time.Duration) (Context, Can-
celFunc) {
	return WithDeadline(parent, time.Now().Add(timeout))
}
```

Here are the best practices when using context:

- **Avoid using `Background()`**: We should aim to start a new context from the parent context and not use the **`context.Background()`**. We don't want to break the current lifecycle and start a new one. We usually use this function at the start of a program.
- **Concurrency best practices**: Will be discussed in the next chapters.
- **Pass context explicitly**: We should strive to pass it as an argument between functions and not use it as a global variable.
- **Prefer Cancel over Timeout**: We always strive to use manual cancellation rather than automatic cancellation. Manual vs. automatic cancellation is the difference between **`context.WithCancel`** and **`context.WithTimeout`**.

All of these best practices lead us to perform propagation of context.

Context propagation involves consistently transferring contextual information, typically through function arguments, to maintain relevant data throughout the execution of a program or system. Context propagation ensures the seamless flow of contextual details across different parts of the code.

We must avoid global environment variables or repeatedly passing the same field or struct through many functions. Context propagation creates a hierarchy between the different logics in the code. For instance, if we process an event, this event triggers several other child events. The child events need all the key-value items from the parent context, but each child event requires a different timeout. This example proves that hierarchy is crucial.

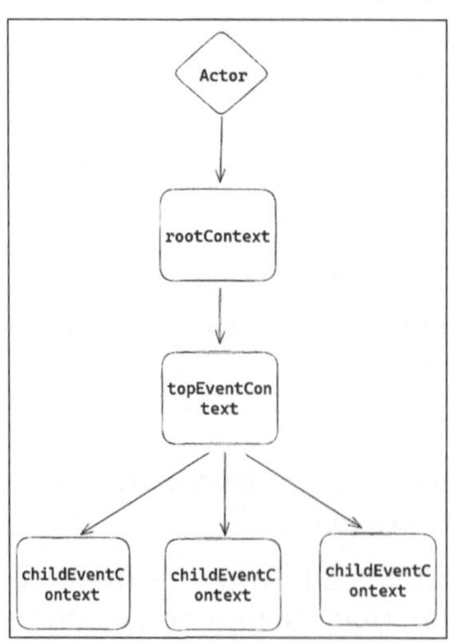

Figure 4.1: *Context propagation*

This hierarchy helps us to control the lifecycles error handling between goroutines.

As discussed, the Go team invented the language intended to run on the cloud. With that thought in mind, context is critical here. When working in a cloud environment, communication between services is often. It becomes more often in Microservices' architecture.

In Microservices architecture, each service relies upon dependencies from others or third-party services. Propagation of context is essential to transfer this information, which can be authentication and authorization data, observability data (tracing, logs), request metadata, and so on.

Errors – Talking About Error Propagation

Error handling is critical and essential to any programming language. This section will discuss the usage and implementation of error handling using Golang.

Error handling in Go is essential, particularly when developing code within a microservices' architecture. Why is that?

When we encounter bugs (which will happen a lot), we must prepare and set the proper infrastructure to investigate the bug. The most annoying thing is to be blind when investigating a bug. The best preparation we can do while writing code is to perform satisfying error handling.

Sometimes, an error can be propagated between many services – for example, a service calling an internal API that fails (because of its internal reason). At first look, the bug is in the service, but actually, the bug is the API. We can understand it quickly if the error handling is done right!

The default error value in Go is `nil,` `error` is a type in Go. There are three ways to create an error type in Go:

The first way is to use the `fmt` package like this:

```
err := fmt.Errorf("a height of %0.2f is invalid", -2.3333)

fmt.Println(err.Error()) // a height of -2.33 is invalid
```

The example is straightforward. For struct to be an error type, it must include a method on the `error` type, which has a signature of - `Error().` This function returns the error as a string. Notice to use it only when you know the error isn't nil. Otherwise, it will panic. The second way to create an error in Go is to use the `errors` package like this:

```
err = errors.New("this is an invalid height")

fmt.Println(err.Error()) // this is an invalid height
```

It has the same effect as the first example but is leaner. There are sensations where it is a convention to use this style rather than the first one. We will elaborate on that convention in the following sections. The third way to create an error in Go is through a custom error type. We would need to declare a struct, and this struct should have a method called **Error()** that returns a string. Let's observe an example:

```
type ApiError struct {
	Path       string
	StatusCode int
}

func (e *ApiError) Error() string {
	return fmt.Sprintf("API error: %s returned a %d", e.Path,
e.StatusCode)
}

func main() {
	err = &ApiError{Path: "/api/users", StatusCode: 500}
	fmt.Println(err.Error()) // API error: /api/users returned a 500
}
```

Error handling is a vast topic, and we will not cover this topic in detail. Instead, we will focus on the following:

- Why error handling in Go differs from other languages
- Errors are here to tell a story
- Conventions

If you want to explore error handling, there is an excellent article about Rob Pike about error handling, which is attached in the references.

In the second chapter, Usability of Go, we elaborated on the mentioned sections. These sections are just a reminder. Note that we won't talk here about panic and recovery; instead, we will talk about them in the following chapters.

Error Handling: Difference between Go and Other Languages

Error handling in Go is different. The Go team took a different approach regarding that. Most of the languages include **try-catch-finally**. Errors will eventually happen, as we all know. Sooner or later, we must consider how we will handle them. Due to excellent error handling, developers can't forget to handle the error and return the precise error message.

Usually, many error messages in other programming languages get swallowed between heaps of `try-catch`. Go gives us a very convenient way to do multi-value returns, which makes our lives easier to return errors properly.

Errors are Here to Tell a Story

In *Chapter 2, Usability of Go*, we talked about "*telling a story*" using errors in Go. Telling a story becomes a force multiplier when we speak in the context of microservices. Because a story of a single service might be simple, but the story of an error across many services will be much more complex. We can resolve it by using tracing between services. We will talk more in detail about tracing in *Chapter 9, Deploying to Production*. In short, tracing is the tracking code between services and errors in particular.

Conventions

We took this conventions table from the Uber-Go convention, and it describes very well the conventions around the guidance on when to use this error and another.

Error matching?	Error Message	Guidance	Description
No	Static	errors.New	A function that creates a new error with the given message.
No	Dynamic	fmt.Errorf	A function that generates formatted error messages
Yes	Static	Top-level var with errors.New	Defines top-level variable with error message using errors. New
Yes	Dynamic	Custom error type	Defining a custom error type

Table 4.1: *Error handling conventions*

Testing - Best Practices, Mocking, and Fuzzy Tests

One of the things we significantly love about Go is that the `testing` package is a core package maintained by the Go team. We encountered many other situations in other languages where we were frustrated to find the proper testing framework because there were so many of them, and each missed something. Our recommendation is to try to avoid using an external testing framework.

This section will discuss what tests look like in Go, how they differ from other languages, and Go tests' best practices.

Note that tests are an enormous topic, and we don't aim to learn about it. Unit tests, component tests, integration tests, smoke tests, mock, stub, fake, and spy are examples of terms and definitions in the testing ecosystem. We aim to learn about the adjustment to Go and the benefits of tests, particularly in Go. Also, we will learn what we need to test when building microservices' architecture.

Our perspective about testing in general goes like this:

1. Tests must be independent.
2. Flaky tests are any system's disease – tests must be reproducible.
3. Tests are a great way to document our code.

What are the steps to create a test in Go and where?

1. Create a file with a postfix of **`_test.go`**. The file can be near the tested file (see the example in this chapter's code). We can create the file in a specific directory for tests.
2. In the test file, declare a function that her signature should be like that `func` **`TestName(t *testing.T)`**. Replace the `Name` with what you want to test. Usually, we test a function, and the `Name` is the function's name. But, the `Test` prefix is necessary.
3. Use the Go CLI to run the test by running - **`go test ./`**

We have a function called get bigger ("**`example.go`**")

```
func GetBigger(a, b float64) float64 {
	return math.Max(a, b)
}
```

And this is how the testing file should look like (**`example_test.go`**):

```
package main


import "testing"


func TestGetBigger(t *testing.T) {
	type args struct {
		a float64
		b float64
	}
```

```
	tests := []struct {
		name string
		args args
		want float64
	}{
		{
			name: "a is the bigger one",
			args: args{
				a: 9,
				b: 6,
			},
			want: 9,
		},
		{
			name: "b is the bigger one",
			args: args{
				a: 3,
				b: 7,
			},
			want: 7,
		},
	}
	for _, tt := range tests {
		t.Run(tt.name, func(t *testing.T) {
			if got := GetBigger(tt.args.a, tt.args.b); got !=
			tt.want {
				t.Errorf("GetBigger() = %v, want %v", got,
				tt.want)
			}
		})
	}
}
```

There are many utilities under the testing function that help us to perform more precise tests. There is a link to a more detailed article about the testing package in Go.

Mocking

This is a valuable tool that helps us set consts for our tests, something that is immutable. We can mock data, and we can mock a function. There are various ways to mock data; the most convenient way is using a `gofakeit` package. It is a very convenient package that helps us to mock data. Let's discuss the mocking function.

We can't mock functions directly in Go. What we actually can `mock` is interfaces. Before mocking an interface, we must know how to mock a **`struct`**. To mock a **`struct`** in Go, we need the struct to be compatible with an interface, and then we can mock that interface. We will see in a second how to do it.

Before that, we will mock a function. To mock a function, as you probably guessed, we need to assign a function to a struct. Here, we can leverage the existence of the empty struct (**`struct{}`**). Here is a use case where we have a function calling another two functions.

```
// Valid name is between 8 and 16 chars and doesn't contain number
func IsValidName(name string) bool {
	numbersValid := IsNumbersValid(name)
	lengthValid := IsLengthValid(name)
	return numbersValid && lengthValid
}

func IsNumbersValid(name string) bool {
	return !strings.ContainsAny(name, "0123456789")
}

func IsLengthValid(name string) bool {
	length := len(name)
	return length >= 8 && length <= 16
}
```

Let's say that we want to create a test for **`IsValidName`** function, but we want to mock **`IsNumbersValid`** and **`IsLengthValid`** functions. The first step is to create an interface and empty **`struct`** as follows:

```
type ValidationClient struct{}
```

```
type ValidationClientInter interface {
	IsNumbersValid(name string) bool
	IsLengthValid(name string) bool
}
```

Then, assign the function that we want to mock to our **struct**.

```
func (c *ValidationClient) IsNumbersValid(name string) bool {
	return !strings.ContainsAny(name, "0123456789")
}

func (c *ValidationClient) IsLengthValid(name string) bool {
	length := len(name)
	return length >= 8 && length <= 16
}
```

After that, we should create an instance of the struct and use that instance to call the function that we want to mock.

```
var Client ValidationClientInter = &ValidationClient{}

func IsValidName(name string) bool {
	numbersValid := Client.IsNumbersValid(name)
	lengthValid := Client.IsLengthValid(name)
	return numbersValid && lengthValid
}
```

Following the example, now we have a function **IsValidName** calling another two functions through a struct client (**Client**), which fulfills an interface.

ValidationClientInter.

Remember that we must have that interface. That is because, in Go, we can use composition to "`override`" an interface. After that, let's use a tool called **mockery**. **mockery** helps us generate mocks by running a command. There is an alternative called **gomock**, which is also very popular in Go. To run **mockery**, use the following command:

```
mockery --all --inpackage
```

This will generate a separate file for each interface. When running this command, the tool will create this file - **mock_ValidationClientInter.go**. The only thing that remains now is to determine the behavior of the mocked function and then assign the `Client` to the mocked client we created before. By doing so, when running the test, it will use the mocked client and not the original client.

```
mockedClient := &MockValidationClientInter{}
mockedClient.On("IsNumbersValid", mock.Anything).Return(true)
mockedClient.On("IsLengthValid", mock.Anything).Return(true)
Client = mockedClient
```

This functionality is happening within the test file.

Fuzzy Testing

Fuzz tests generate input for a function using supplied seed data. Fuzz testing proves to be an effective method for uncovering unforeseen behaviors within our code. It helps to find where the code could panic so we can handle this particular use case we didn't think of.

Fuzzing is a new capability in Go. Support fuzzing testing from version 1.18. Let's look at a simple function parsing string into first and last names.

```
// ParseName parses a name into first and last.
func ParseName(s string) (string, string, error) {
	parts := strings.Split(s, " ")
	return parts[0], parts[1], nil
}
```

We created a fuzz test for this function like this:

```
func FuzzParseName(f *testing.F) {
	f.Add("John Adams")
	f.Add("George Washington")
	f.Fuzz(func(t *testing.T, s string) {
		_, _, err := ParseName(s)
		if err != nil {
			t.Errorf("%v", err)
		}
	})
}
```

Now, let's run the fuzzing test with a timeout of 12 seconds. Note that fuzzing test timeout is infinite (because it always tries to find more use cases). We can run the fuzzing test by running the following command:

```
go test -fuzz FuzzParseName -fuzztime=12s
```

After running this command, we encountered a panic error:

```
panic: runtime error: index out of range [1] with length 1
```

Pretty straightforward, the reason for the panic is that we didn't check a case of a string that is empty or doesn't contain space. To solve it, we need to handle that use case. Also, ignore the new error type in the test.

```
var ErrInvalidName = errors.New("invalid name")


// ParseName parses a name into first and last.
func ParseName(s string) (string, string, error) {
	parts := strings.Split(s, " ")
	if len(parts) != 2 {
		return "", "", ErrInvalidName
	}
	return parts[0], parts[1], nil
}


func FuzzParseName(f *testing.F) {
	f.Add("John Adams")
	f.Add("George Washington")
	f.Fuzz(func(t *testing.T, s string) {
		_, _, err := ParseName(s)
		if err != nil {
			if errors.Is(err, ErrInvalidName) {
				return
			}
			t.Errorf("%v", err)
		}
	})
}
```

Note the fuzzing test must have the prefix of **Fuzz** in the test name.

Microservices Testing

Microservices, by their inherent design, are characterized as being straightforward and self-contained. Following the adapter design pattern, we should encapsulate inter-service communication by wrapping the HTTP client. There is a reference to this design pattern to read further in the References section.

While creating the custom client (wrapped client) that communicates to the other services, we should strive to create those clients as structs. The structs must implement an interface. There are two best practices regarding using clients' interfaces in microservices:

- Each service client has its interface - higher flexibility and more work.
- All services have a common interface - lower flexibility and less work.

The reason why we need an interface (regardless of the option we chose) is to have the ability to mock the clients' responses, as we saw in the preceding sections ("*Mocking*"). We would like to mock the client response when writing tests in the scope of a single service.

A more powerful kind of test is inter-services. Although it is much more powerful, it also takes a lot of time and effort to do it. There are endless theories regarding those kinds of inter-service tests. The main aspect is to set the **`Setup`** and **`Teardown`** of those tests properly while ensuring that those kinds of tests are reproducible. Commonly, those tests become flaky in nimbleness. We should aspire to use the **`Functional Options Pattern`** we saw in this chapter. In an optimal scenario, the `Setup` function should look like defining many `Options` (basically, configuration).

Two relevant efficacious tools Golang brings when discussing building microservices architects in Go are:

- Performing benchmark
- Race Detector

Performing Benchmark

The benchmark is a built-in option in the test CLI. Benchmark helps us to test the performance of a function. Benchmarking is a powerful methodology that helps us to achieve good performance. Building microservices can be even more powerful because we can investigate specific endpoints when they become slow. Let's see how we can perform a benchmark test.

```
func Fib(n int) int {
	if n < 2 {
		return n
	}
	return Fib(n-1) + Fib(n-2)
}
```

And we want to see what the performance of this function for large inputs is. We need to create a test function with the prefix **`Benchmark`** and a signature that looks like that **`(b *testing.B)`**, then the test should look like this:

```
func BenchmarkFib(b *testing.B) {
        for n := 0; n < b.N; n++ {
                Fib(20)
        }
}
```

To run the benchmark, we need to use the Go CLI as follows:

```
go test -bench=.
```

There are various configurations for running benchmark tests that can be explored.

Race Detector

In the Go CLI, a built-in option lets us detect race conditions. A race condition is a frequent situation that happens a lot in microservices systems. Furthermore, it can happen easily in Go due to their concurrency approach. The race detector can run against the executable program or the tests. Let's see an example where we are running a race detector against a simple case:

```
func main() {
        i := 0
        go func() {
                i++
        }()
        fmt.Println(i)
}
```

In the preceding example, a goroutine has been called in the second line of the function. When we print **`i,`** we can get two options: **`0`** or **`1`**. The reason for that is a race condition. We don't know if the goroutine will finish until the **`Println`** is called because they run in parallel. The command we can use to run the race detector is:

```
go run -race race-detector.go
```

We will accept a warning

```
==================
WARNING: DATA RACE
Write at 0x00c00011a028 by goroutine 6:
  main.main.func1()
```

```
        /Users/nirshtein/Documents/GitHub/Microservices-with-Go/chap-
ter-5/race-detector/race-detector.go:8 +0x3c


Previous read at 0x00c00011a028 by main goroutine:
  main.main()
        /Users/nirshtein/Documents/GitHub/Microservices-with-Go/chap-
ter-5/race-detector/race-detector.go:10 +0xa8


Goroutine 6 (running) created at:
  main.main()
        /Users/nirshtein/Documents/GitHub/Microservices-with-Go/chap-
ter-5/race-detector/race-detector.go:7 +0x9c
==================
Found 1 data race(s)
exit status 66
```

The warning is unequivocal. It is recommended to explore the variety of configurations to detect race conditions in Go. The next chapters will discuss techniques to resolve these race conditions.

Conclusion

In this chapter, we discussed the language's core pillars. Each one of those topics is much bigger than the things we discussed. We encourage you to continue to explore each one of those pillars. The references in this chapter are a great starting point.

The next chapter will discuss one of the main pillars of the language - Concurrency!

References

- https://refactoring.guru/design-patterns/go
- https://go.dev/blog/errors-are-values
- https://github.com/brianvoe/gofakeit
- https://go.dev/security/fuzz/
- https://refactoring.guru/design-patterns/adapter/go/example
- https://pkg.go.dev/testing#hdr-Benchmarks
- https://go.dev/blog/race-detector

CHAPTER 5
Unlocking Go's Concurrency Power

Introduction

In the previous chapter, we delved into essential topics within Go and this language's basic principles. This chapter will focus on and delve into the most prominent pillar - Concurrency. One core motivation behind Go's development is to give developers a straightforward and convenient way to write code that runs concurrently. We will cover all the Go-related topics in concurrency - Goroutines, channels, principles, design patterns, concurrency pitfalls like goroutine leaks, and more. Concurrency aims to deliver optimal performance. Good performance is a key indicator of any type of architecture, primarily for microservices.

In *Chapter 2*, *Usability of Go*, we discussed how goroutines and the scheduler work. We will continue from there and elaborate on goroutines in this chapter. Before we jump into concurrency in Golang, let's address three potentially confusing terms:

- Concurrency
- Parallelism
- Asynchronism

Concurrency is when the execution of multiple tasks is interleaved instead of each task being executed sequentially, one after another.

Parallelism is when these tasks are actually being executed in parallel.

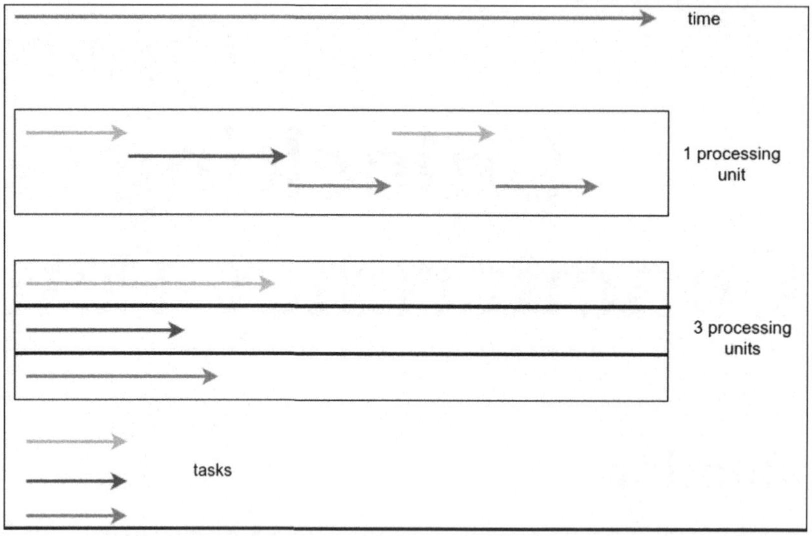

Figure 5.1: *Concurrency and parallelism comparison*

Asynchrony is a separate concept (even though related in some contexts). One event might happen at a different time (not synchrony) to another. The following diagrams illustrate the difference between a synchronous and an asynchronous execution, where the actors can correspond to other threads, processes, or even servers.

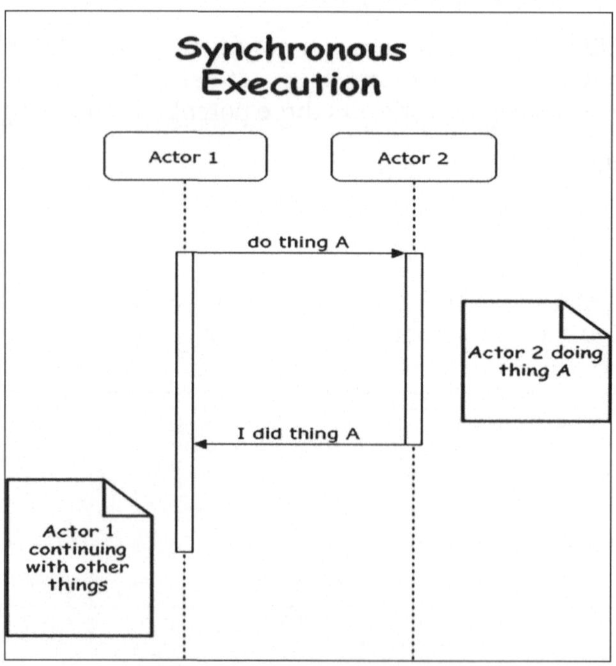

Figure 5.2: *Synchronous process*

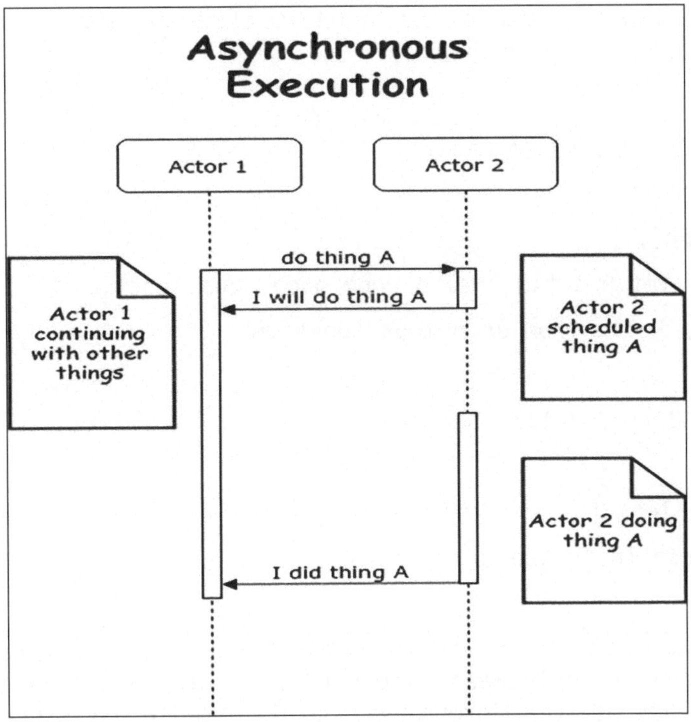

Figure 5.3: *Asynchronous process*

It is essential to note the difference because, in this chapter, we will talk about concurrency in Go.

Structure

In this chapter, we will discuss the following topics:

- Goroutines
- Channels - Buffered vs. Unbuffered
- **Sync** Package
- Pub/Sub
- Channel Closing Principle
- Avoiding Goroutine Leak
- Fan In Fan Out Pattern

Goroutines

Goroutines and channels are the core concepts we use in Go to implement concurrency. In this section, we will explore code examples demonstrating the execution of Goroutines, examine the limitations of running Goroutines, and discuss the implications of Goroutine leaks.

```
func main() {
	go printHello() // Hello

	go func() {
		fmt.Println("Hello from anonymous function")
	}() // Hello from anonymous function

	time.Sleep(1 * time.Second)
}
func printHello() {
	fmt.Println("Hello")
}
```

It is as simple as that just use the keyword **go** and then call a function. The function can be declared like **printHello** and can be an anonymous function. The Go scheduler will manage the Goroutines from the moment we execute them. The scheduler is responsible for allocating new goroutines, assigning them to a thread, executing them, pausing if needed, communicating between them, and deallocating goroutines.

A prevalent question is the maximum amount of goroutines we can run in Go. The answer is that it depends. A reminder from *Chapter 2, Usability of Go* - behind the senses, we have threads managed by the Go scheduler. The **GOMAXPROCS** configures the number of threads; the default and recommended value is the number of cores of the machine we are running on. Hypothetically, we can run as many goroutines as we want, but we must consider two factors - memory usage and garbage collection performance.

Memory usage – Each goroutine uses 2KB, which means a 1GB memory machine can hold a maximum of ~250K goroutines. We need to calculate the maximum number of goroutines for every machine we are running on.

GC performance - As many goroutines we have, garbage collection will become slower and slower.

A rule of thumb for the maximum goroutines is between 1000 and 10,000.

So, what is a goroutine leak? A goroutine leak is when garbage is never collected because it sends or waits to receive data over channels. Let's discuss channels first and get real-life examples of goroutines leaks.

Channels - Buffered vs. Unbuffered

The best way to describe channels is that they are like queues. Their behavior is similar to queues – we can send and receive items into them. The difference between queues and channels is that channels aim to facilitate goroutine communication. Channels are how goroutines communicate and send and receive data between them.

Here is an example where we create a channel, send data to that channel, and then receive the data in the main goroutines from the same channel:

```
func main() {
	messages := make(chan string)

	go func() {
		messages <- "ping"
	}()

	msg := <-messages
	println(msg)
}
```

We use the **chan** keyword to declare a channel. Note that each channel has a type. In the example, the channel is of type **string**, which means we can only send items from **string** type to it. Using the syntax of **<-**, we send the `ping` string into the channel. We receive the data onto the channel using the assigning syntax **:=** and the **<-** syntax.

In the preceding example, we used an unbuffered channel.

There are two types of channels in Golang: buffered and unbuffered channels. Let's examine the difference between them.

```
func main() {
	messages := make(chan string, 2)

	messages <- "ping"
	messages <- "pong"

	println(<-messages) // ping
	println(<-messages) // pong
}
```

To declare a buffered channel, we should use the following syntax: **make(chan type, int)**.

The `int` is the size of the channel. As we saw, channels are like queues. The size of the channel is the size of the queue, which means we can't send more items into the channel than its size unless there is a receiver on the other side. Note that the output is like a queue order, not a stack order (FIFO, not LIFO).

We will block the code if we try to send an item into a full channel. Unless there is a receiver goroutine - it will unblock the sender goroutine. If all other goroutines remain, we will enter a deadlock, and Go will notify us.

```
func main() {
        messages := make(chan string, 1)

        messages <- "ping"
        messages <- "pong"

        println(<-messages)
        println(<-messages)
}
```

The only thing we changed is the size of the channel. However, if we try to run this code, we will get the following error:

```
fatal error: all goroutines are asleep - deadlock!
```

We got this error because we tried to send an item to the full channel while no goroutine ran a receiver that was supposed to unblock the main code. Now, let's take an example of an unbuffered channel.

```
func main() {
        messages := make(chan string)

        go func() {
                messages <- "ping"
        }()

        msg := <-messages
        println(msg)
}
```

The way to declare an unbuffered channel is exactly like a buffered channel, just without declaring the size. The difference between them is that the unbuffered channel has 0 length. While using unbuffered channels and buffered channels that are full, we can't send items to the channel (**chan <-**) without having a corresponding receiver (**<- chan**).

Closing a Channel

When we create channels, they are, by default, open. We can use the **close(channel)** syntax to close a channel. Closing a channel means we can't send data into the channel, but we can still receive data.

```
func main() {
        ch := make(chan int)
        close(ch)
        ch <- 1 // panic: send on closed channel
}
```

The purpose of closing a channel is to notify the receiver that the sender has finished its work and won't send any more items. Note that closing a channel must happen only from the sender side and not from the receiver side. We will discuss the principle of closing channels in more detail in the later section.

Range Over a Channel

We already saw the usage of the **range** syntax. We can use the same syntax for iterating over values from a channel, such as the receiver side.

```
func main() {
        ch := make(chan int, 3)
        for i := 0; i < 3; i++ {
                ch <- i
        }
        close(ch) // if you don't close the channel, deadlock will occur
        for i := range ch {
                fmt.Printf("%d ", i) // 0 1 2
        }
}
```

In the example, we send three items to the channels and then iterate over the received values through the **range** syntax.

Please note two things.

First, we must close the channel; it will lead to deadlock! The **range-for-loop** will be stuck forever if we don't close the channel. The sender doesn't notify the receiver that he has finished sending items.

Second, closing a channel prevents data from being sent to the channel. It doesn't prevent receiving data from the channel like we did in the last three lines in the example.

Selecting a Channel

We already saw the usage of the **select** syntax. We can use the same syntax for receiving data from multiple channels.

```
func main() {
        c1 := make(chan int)
        c2 := make(chan int)
        go func() {
                c1 <- 1
        }()
        go func() {
                c2 <- 2
        }()

        go func() {
                for {
                        select {
                        case <-c1:
                                println("c1")
                        case <-c2:
                                println("c2")
                        }
                }
        }()

        time.Sleep(1 * time.Second)
}
```

The two goroutines can send data over the respective channels anytime. We need a single mechanism on the other side that will know to receive data from multiple channels. The **select** syntax is the solution for that use case. We can see how to leverage it in the example.

Channels Directions

We can specify the channel direction while using channels as function parameters.

```
func main() {
	ch := make(chan int, 1)

	send(ch)
	recv(ch)
}

func send(ch chan<- int) {
	ch <- 1
}

func recv(ch <-chan int) {
	fmt.Println(<-ch) // 1
}
```

We used the syntax of **chan<-** to specify that we can receive a channel as a parameter, but we can only send data onto that channel.

Synchronization Between Goroutines

One of the most useful use cases of channels is synchronization. We can synchronize between goroutines by notifying them about a process's start and end through channels. A pervasive pattern to notify of work that is "**done**" between goroutines is to use a boolean channel of size 1.

```
func main() {
	done := make(chan bool, 1)

	go func() {
		println("Start goroutine")
		time.Sleep(1 * time.Second) // simulate work
		println("End goroutine")
		done <- true
```

```
    }()

    println("Waiting goroutine")
    <-done

    println("All done")
}
```

Leveraging Channel Strength

The usage of channels, as we saw, is communication between goroutines. There are several use cases for leveraging channel strength:

- Synchronization between goroutines
- Sending and receiving notification
- Accepting data from several goroutines using **select**
- Futures and promises **->** mimicking the process **async/await**
- Acting as queues
- Timeouts
- Handling a fatal
- Ticker
- Fan In Fan Out pattern

These are a few leading examples of use cases. There are many more use cases and examples.

When should we use buffered channels, and when should we use unbuffered channels?

By default, we should opt for unbuffered channels. Buffered channels become necessary when the receiver lags behind the sender, or synchronization is required before data retrieval. These are the primary reasons for using buffered channels over unbuffered channels. Additionally, specific program requirements may also dictate the use of buffered/unbuffered channels.

Sync Package

The **sync** package is one of the core packages in Go. This package provides basic synchronization primitives. Most of the types in the package provide low-level routines. Higher-lever routines should be performed via channels.

WaitGroups

WaitGroup is a type in the **sync** package. **WaitGroup** provides a way to wait for multiple goroutines to finish their work. It is an immensely potent tool with widespread usage.

```
func main() {
	wg := sync.WaitGroup{}
	wg.Add(5)

	for i := 0; i < 5; i++ {
		go func(i int) {
			defer wg.Done()
			time.Sleep(1 * time.Second)
			println(i)
		}(i)
	}

	fmt.Println("Waiting...")
	wg.Wait()
	fmt.Println("Done")
}
```

The output will look like this (the order of the numbers can change):

```
Waiting...
2
0
1
3
4
Done
```

WaitGroup type works as a counter. Behind the senses, the **WaitGroup** type holds a counter int type, and the initialized value is 0. All the goroutines blocked on the **Wait()** are released if the counter value becomes 0. We used the **Add(delta int)** function to increment the counter size. To decrease the counter's value, we used the function **Done()** - which subtracts 1 from the counter. These are all the methods on the **WaitGroup** type - **Add, Done, Wait**.

Note that a negative value in the **Add** function will lead to panic. Also, if we pass the **WaitGroup** instance between functions, we should do it by pointer.

The biggest disadvantage of this technique is that there isn't a conventional way to handle errors. There is a separate package called **errgroup**, which helps us to achieve that.

Locks

To access the same data across several goroutines, we need to protect access to the data from one goroutine while the other is accessing it. Such a scenario can cause faulty data or, even worse - fatal errors.

```
func main() {
	counter := 0
	wg := sync.WaitGroup{}
	wg.Add(10000)

	for i := 0; i < 10000; i++ {
		go func() {
			defer wg.Done()
			counter++
		}()
	}

	wg.Wait()
	fmt.Println("counter:", counter)
}
```

In the preceding example, the output of the counter should be 10,000. Unfortunately, the counter is somewhere under it. The reason is that multiple goroutines try to access the counter variable; some fail because other goroutines lock the counter value and write to it. If we replace the counter with a map and try to write to the same key, we will get an even worse scenario - a **fatal error: concurrent map writes**. To avoid this situation, we need to use **mutex**. **Mutex** is a **sync** package type that helps us lock and unlock.

```
func main() {
	counter := 0
	wg := sync.WaitGroup{}
	mu := sync.Mutex{}
```

```
	wg.Add(10000)

	for i := 0; i < 10000; i++ {
		go func() {
			defer wg.Done()
			mu.Lock()
			counter++
			mu.Unlock()
		}()
	}

	wg.Wait()
	fmt.Println("counter:", counter)
}
```

Now the output will be - **`counter: 10000`**, as expected. The `mutex` type lets us lock. For any other goroutine wanting to **`Lock()`** the mutex (**`mu`**), we must wait until another goroutine **`Unlock()`** the mutex (**`mu`**).

Singleton in Golang - `Once.Do`

Summing up the concept of a singleton - it's among the most recognized design patterns for guaranteeing the creation of a single instance of a specific type. In many other programming languages, various patterns exist to achieve this while maintaining thread safety. In Go, it is super easy to implement this pattern while using the **`Once`** type from the **`sync`** package.

```
type cache struct{}

var cacheSingleton *cache

var once sync.Once

func main() {
	GetCache()
	GetCache()
	GetCache()
}
```

```
func GetCache() *cache {
        once.Do(func() {
                println("Creating singleton object")
                cacheSingleton = &cache{}
        })
        return cacheSingleton
}
```

The output of this program is - **`Creating singleton object`**. And that's it (not three times).

The **`Do`** function receives a function as a parameter. The **`Do`** function ensures that the function inside is executed exactly once, which we want to achieve when writing a singleton. **`Do`** is also the only function that exists on the `Once` type.

Low-Level Routines

There are other low-level routines we can use in the **`sync`** package that we won't elaborate on in this chapter:

1. **`sync.Map`**: The same purpose as the normal map in Go but is safe for concurrent access across several goroutines.
2. **`sync/atomic`**: Managing shared counter state across several goroutines.
3. **`sync.Pool`**: Self-managed temporary retrieval object pool – this is to facilitate the Garbage Collector work.

Pub/Sub

Publish-subscribe is one of the most known patterns. Pub/Sub pattern is a messaging pattern that helps us to communicate between systems/services/objects. It broadcasts data/messages from what is called a publisher through a topic. Each subscriber is allocated to a specific topic, and every subscriber receives all the messages associated with the topic to which they are assigned.

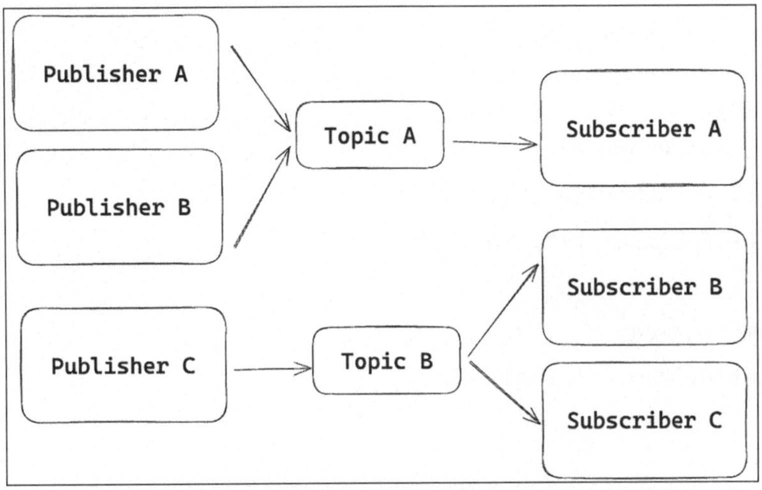

***Figure 5.4**: Publish-Subscribe pattern*

```
type PubSub struct {
	subscribers map[string][]chan interface{}
}

func NewPubSub() *PubSub {
	return &PubSub{
		subscribers: make(map[string][]chan interface{}),
	}
}

func (ps *PubSub) Publish(topic string, item interface{}) {
	for _, ch := range ps.subscribers[topic] {
		ch <- item
	}
}

func (ps *PubSub) Subscribe(topic string) <-chan interface{} {
	ch := make(chan interface{})
	ps.subscribers[topic] = append(ps.subscribers[topic], ch)

	return ch
```

```
}

func main() {
	ps := NewPubSub()
	ch := ps.Subscribe("t1")
	go ps.Publish("t1", "hello")

	item := <-ch
	println(item.(string))
}
```

This is a simple implementation of the publish-subscribe pattern in Go. Note that this example is imperfect - we don't close the channels and do not handle concurrency properly. Utilizing existing libraries is the suggested approach when implementing this pattern.

Pub/Sub is a pattern in microservices architecture. When building microservices architecture, each service works independently and decouples from one another, which is precisely what the Pub/Sub pattern aims to do. It allows writing each subscriber independently without changing the publisher code to get his data. He just needs to assign himself to an existing topic. Numerous advantages of microservices architecture are reflected in this pattern. One major example is the scalability of the services that become seamless while using Pub/Sub.

More advanced Pub/Sub usage allows several more capabilities such as scheduled processes, delays, workflows, and so on. Here are some real-life examples of using Pub/Sub:

- Broadcast of event data
- Real-time notifications
- Distributed caching
- Live location tracking

Note that to use Pub/Sub between services in microservices architecture, we need to use a third service that manages the topics, publishers, and subscribers. Familiar technologies for Pub/Sub can be found as a service in all the biggest cloud vendors or open-source projects like Redis.

Many people tend to confuse Pub/Sub to Message Broker. Let's see the difference between them in a nutshell.

PubSub	Message Broker
Like broadcast - single message copies to many subscribers	Unicast - single message to a single consumer
Publisher and Subscriber	Publisher and Consumer
Ideal for broadcasting	Ideal for task delegation
More susceptible to message loss	More resilient and have better reliability
No FIFO capability	Have FIFO capability - to keep order

***Table 5.1** : Comparison between PubSub and Message Broker*

We will discuss message brokers more in detail in *Chapter 7, Building RESTful* API.

Channel Closing Principle

We already mentioned the channel closing principle in a nutshell. However, it is so important that we need to discuss it again. The simple principle says we must close a channel from the sender goroutine if this is a single sender. We shouldn't close channels from the receiver side and shouldn't close channels from the sender side if we have several senders.

Although the principle is there are scenarios where we need to close the channel from multiple senders. In that scenario, we must perform a graceful close if we have multiple senders and need to close the channel.

```
func main() {
	ch := make(chan int)
	wg := &sync.WaitGroup{}
	wg.Add(10)
	for i := 0; i < 10; i++ {
		go Sender(ch, wg, i)
	}

	go func() {
		wg.Wait()
		close(ch) // graceful close
	}()

	// receiver
```

```
        for i := range ch {
                println(i)
        }
}

func Sender(ch chan<- int, wg *sync.WaitGroup, i int) {
        defer wg.Done()
        ch <- i
}
```

In the preceding example, we can observe a graceful channel close with multiple sender goroutines.

Avoiding Goroutine Leak

Until now, we have experienced all the good that goroutines offer. Unfortunately, there is a downside of goroutines - goroutine leak!

A goroutine **`leak`** can happen when a sender goroutine is blocked until the receiver arrives at the channel and vice versa. Meanwhile, the blocked goroutine never gets unblocked.

```
func leak(ch chan int) {
        data := <-ch
        fmt.Println(data)
}

func main() {
        ch := make(chan int)

        go leak(ch)
}
```

Let's take a look at the preceding example; how is that a leak? It is a goroutine leak because we don't have a receiver! The `leak` function is stuck forever.

There are two common situations where goroutines can occur:

- Forgotten sender
- Abandoned receiver

Forgotten Sender

This is a scenario where a sender goroutine is being "**forgotten**" and tries to send data via a channel. However, there is no receiver on the other side.

```
func forgottenSender(ch chan int) {
	data := 3
	// This is blocked as no one is receiving the data
	ch <- data
}

func main() {
	ch := make(chan int)
	go forgottenSender(ch)
	println(runtime.NumGoroutine()) // 2 instead of 1
}
```

The **forgottenSender** function will keep running within a goroutine forever. In this example, we must use a buffered channel to avoid a goroutine leak so the **forgottenSender** could finish its work.

```
func forgottenSender(ch chan int) {
	data := 3
	// This is blocked as no one is receiving the data
	ch <- data
}

func main() {
	ch := make(chan int, 1) // avoid goroutine leak by using buffered
	channel
	go forgottenSender(ch)
}
```

It isn't always outward that there is a goroutine leak. We can see many scenarios where error handling can cause unintentional goroutine leaks.

```
func networkCall() int {
	return 1
}
```

```
func anotherAction() error {
	return errors.New("data is invalid! Returning")
}

func forgottenSender(ch chan int) {
	data := networkCall()

	ch <- data
}

func handler() error {
	ch := make(chan int)
	go forgottenSender(ch)

	err := anotherAction()
	if err != nil {
		return err
	}

	data := <-ch
	fmt.Println(data)
	return nil
}
```

Everything will be fine if we eliminate the section where the `anotherAction` function is being called. Unfortunately, let's assume that this code block is necessary. We have a goroutine leak because the `forgottenSender` function keeps running in the background while the handler function returns an error, and now that function has done its work. To solve this situation, we must run the receiver in a goroutine before calling the `anotherAction` function or use a buffered channel.

Akin to the error handling use case, it can also happen when we use a select case for multiple channels.

```
func networkCall() int {
	time.Sleep(3 * time.Second)
	return 1
```

```
}
func forgottenSender(ch chan int) {
	data := networkCall()
	ch <- data
}

func handler() error {
	ctx, cancel := context.WithTimeout(context.Background(), 10*time.
	Millisecond)
	defer cancel()

	ch := make(chan int)
	go forgottenSender(ch)

	for {
		select {
		case data := <-ch:
			fmt.Printf("received data! %d\n", data)
			return nil
		case <-ctx.Done():
			return errors.New("timeout! Process canceled.
			Returning")
		}
	}
}
```

We have the same problem: the handler function finishes its work before the network call is done (the timeout for 10 milliseconds is lower than 3 seconds). The **forgottenSender** function is stuck and doesn't have a receiver on the other side, which leads to a goroutine leak. We can solve this goroutine leak by using a buffered channel.

When we use buffered channels, it unblocks the goroutine, then the GC notices that no one is using the channel **ch** and cleans it from memory.

Abandoned Receiver

This is a scenario where a sender sends data, but the sender never notifies the receiver that he needs to stop receiving data.

```
func abandonedReceiver(ch chan string) {
	for data := range ch {
		println(data)
	}

	println("Worker is done")
}

func sender(ch chan string) {
	for _, data := range []string{"one", "two", "three"} {
		ch <- data
	}
}

func handler() {
	ch := make(chan string, 3)
	sender(ch)

	go abandonedReceiver(ch)

}

func main() {
	handler()
	time.Sleep(1 * time.Second)
	println(runtime.NumGoroutine()) // 2 instead of 1
}
```

As we can see, the **abandonedReceiver** function will keep running forever. The output of the current program will look like this:

```
one
two
three
```

The line "**Worker is done**" will never be printed because the **abandonedReceiver** is blocked on the range for a loop – which causes a goroutine leak. To solve it, we need to close the channel after the sender finishes his job, as we already saw in the section on closing a channel.

```
func sender(ch chan string) {
        for _, data := range []string{"one", "two", "three"} {
                ch <- data
        }
        close(ch) // solve the goroutine leak
}
```

Detecting Goroutine Leak

Let's highlight the fact that a goroutine leak manifests as a memory leak. A goroutine in the background holds variables that aren't being released from memory. There are two primary ways to detect goroutine leaks:

- **Profiling**: We will discuss profiling in more detail in *Chapter* 10, *Next Steps in Production*. Generally, while profiling and analyzing the code, we can check for non-terminated goroutines using the Go profile (pprof) or gops.
- **Tests**: The best but most exhausting way is to write unit tests that reveal goroutine leaks. We aim to cover all the situations where a goroutine leak can happen. The tests inherently check at the end of the test if any goroutines are still running in the background. Go allows us to see how many goroutines run in the background using **runtime.NumGoroutine()**. We can also use an external package like **- uber-go/goleak**.

Fan In Fan Out Pattern

Fan In Fan Out is a popular pattern that helps us handle multiple sources converted into a single stream (fan-in) or input from one source being streamed into multiple pipelines (fan-out). In Go, if we need multiple functions to read from the same channel until the channel is closed - fan out. A single function that can read from multiple inputs (sources) until all the input channels are closed - fan-in.

Fan Out

We should use the fan-out pattern when we want to distribute the work among a group of workers to perform optimization by parallelism to resources like CPU and I/O.

```
func generator(numbers []int) <-chan int {
        out := make(chan int)
```

```
	go func() {
		for _, num := range numbers {
			out <- num
		}
		close(out)
	}()

	return out
}

func businessLogic(num int) int {
	return num * 2
}

func main() {
	data := []int{1, 2, 3, 4, 5, 6}
	var wg sync.WaitGroup

	ch1 := generator(data[0:3])
	ch2 := generator(data[3:])
	wg.Add(2)

	go func() {
		for num := range ch1 {
			println(businessLogic(num))
		}
		wg.Done()
	}()

	go func() {
		for num := range ch2 {
			println(businessLogic(num))
		}
```

```
            wg.Done()
        }()

        wg.Wait()
}
```

In the preceding example, we have a data variable (the source), but we want to parallelize the process of that data. We decided to split the work among two workers. The first thing we did was to split the data into two. Then, we called the **generator** function. The **generator** function's purpose is to accept input, send all the input into a channel called out, and then return that channel. After calling the **generator** function twice, we used **WaitGroup** to wait for all the workers to finish their work. Finally, we executed two goroutines (workers). Each worker performed some business logic and then finished.

Fan In

We should use the fan-in pattern to process multiple inputs (sources) into a single function. We will do it by merging multiple channels into one. The process of combining multiple channels into a single channel is called multiplexing. The single channel will be closed only when all the input channels will be closed. We will examine the multiplexing process by a function called **merge**.

```
func merge(sourcesCh ...<-chan int) <-chan int {
        var wg sync.WaitGroup
        wg.Add(len(sourcesCh))

        out := make(chan int)

        outputFunc := func(sourceCh <-chan int) {
                for num := range sourceCh {
                        out <- num
                }
                wg.Done()
        }

        for _, sourceCh := range sourcesCh {
                go outputFunc(sourceCh)
        }
```

```
	go func() {
		wg.Wait()
		close(out)
	}()

	return out
}

func generator(numbers []int) <-chan int {
	out := make(chan int)
	go func() {
		for _, num := range numbers {
			out <- num
		}
		close(out)
	}()
	return out
}

func main() {
	data := []int{1, 2, 3, 4, 5, 6}

	ch1 := generator(data[0:3])
	ch2 := generator(data[3:])

	ch := merge(ch1, ch2)

	for num := range ch {
		println(num)
	}
}
```

The **generator** function is the same as we saw in the example of the fan-out pattern. We first declare the single output channel called out in the **merge** function. Second, we create a **WaitGroup** to determine when all the multiple source channels are being closed. After they are closed, we will use **`Wait()`** and close the output (**`out`**) channel. Then, we created a function (**`outputFunc`**) that accepts the source channel and sends all the data from that source channel to the output channel (out). Finally, we iterate onto all the source channels and execute the goroutine, called the **`outputFunc`**.

We now have a single channel to iterate safely in the **`main`** function until the **`merge`** function closes the channel.

Conclusion

In this chapter, we talked in detail about concurrency in Go. It is one of the most important topics in Go, and it is crucial to understand it well to write code. In the previous two chapters, we discussed the Go basics topic to have a deep knowledge of how Go works, which is imperative to build a microservices architecture with Go. Throughout these chapters, we had a glimpse of how to leverage Go knowledge into building microservices architecture.

In the next chapter, we will go over the fundamentals elements for building microservices architecture

References

- https://stackoverflow.com/questions/4844637/what-is-the-difference-between-concurrency-parallelism-and-asynchronous-methods#:~:text=Concurrency%20is%20when%20the%20execution,though%20related%20in%20some%20contexts
- https://pkg.go.dev/sync
- https://pkg.go.dev/golang.org/x/sync/errgroup
- https://www.uber.com/en-JO/blog/leakprof-featherlight-in-production-goroutine-leak-detection/#:~:text=A%20possible%20solution%20to%20prevent,a%20buffer%20size%20of%201.
- https://github.com/uber-go/goleak

CHAPTER 6
Core Elements of Microservices

Introduction

After we cover all the essential knowledge related to the Go programming language, we will combine it with the core elements of microservices architecture. You are probably asking yourself what are those "*core elements*"; microservices architecture is an **approach**, not a destination. Therefore, the core elements are tech industry methodologies, design patterns, and technologies. All of those elements together will compose an entire system. There isn't a recipe that tells us how to physique out an architecture. There are many constraints, product requirements (which can drag engineering requirements), and assumptions – each system has its unique structure. However, all these systems have elements in common. This chapter presents those elements, when they can become beneficial, their advantages/disadvantages, and when to use/avoid them. We won't be delving into every single element; instead, the objective is to provide a framework outlining the boundaries of each element.

We will not cover all the existing elements for microservices. Instead, we will go through the leading ones. Here are elements we won't cover in this chapter:

- **Saga Pattern**: Allows us to manage distributed transactions in a microservices architecture by breaking them into smaller, isolated steps, each with its compensating transaction to handle potential failures.
- **Aggregator Pattern**: Reduces data from multiple services to simplify the data for other services that wish to pull it.
- **Decomposition Pattern**: Helps us break monolithic into microservices.
- **Branch Pattern**: Creates separated versions (branches) of the same service. We can perform complex rollouts like blue-green or A/B testing.
- **Service Orchestration**: We will cover this in *Chapter 8, Introduction to Kubernetes.*
- **Design of Failures**: We will cover this in *Chapter 9, Deploying to Production.*
- **Monitoring**: We will cover this in *Chapter 10, Next Steps in Production.*

A final note to acknowledge before starting this chapter is that most of the patterns we will discuss in this chapter have an internal implementation in Kubernetes. Nowadays, using Kubernetes when crafting microservices architecture is an industry standard.

Structure

In this chapter, we will discuss the following topics:

- Communication Between Services
  - API Calls
  - Message Brokers
  - gRPC
- API Gateway
- Service Discovery
- Load Balancer
- Database per Service
- Backends for Frontends (BFF)
- External Configuration
- Service Mesh
- Event-Driven Architecture
  - Event Sourcing
  - CQRS

Communication Between Services

As we saw in *Chapter 1, Introduction to Microservices*, microservices architecture comprises small, independent, and decoupled services. Each service intends to fulfill a **single** purpose. However, the system wants to use all the services to achieve bigger goals. In pursuit of these goals, the services need a means of communication, enabling them to exchange data through sending and receiving. This communication form has many faces due to its complexity.

There are many aspects to consider – message type, message size, response manner, latency, failures, documentation, packing of messages, and more. Following are the leading forms for communicating in a microservices architecture:

- API Calls
- Message Brokers
- gRPC

We won't explore these forms in depth, as each one is vast and requires thorough understanding. To use them correctly and precisely, we must know how to build them correctly. We must also familiarize ourselves with their advantages and disadvantages to make the best decision when choosing between them. Moreover, several other factors, constraints, and assumptions contribute to the situation's complexity.

API Calls

API stands for Application Programming Interface. API calls are composed of requests from the service that sends the call and responses from the services that receive the requests. Each request contains parameters that tell which data is requested. We send API requests over layer 7 of the network, the application layer.

API calls are the most frequent communication approach between services in the microservices architecture. Diverse API styles, such as REST, SOAP, and GraphQL, warrant in-depth discussion. Among them, REST stands out as the most widely adopted. Consequently, the next chapter (*Chapter 7, Building RESTful API*) will explore RESTful APIs.

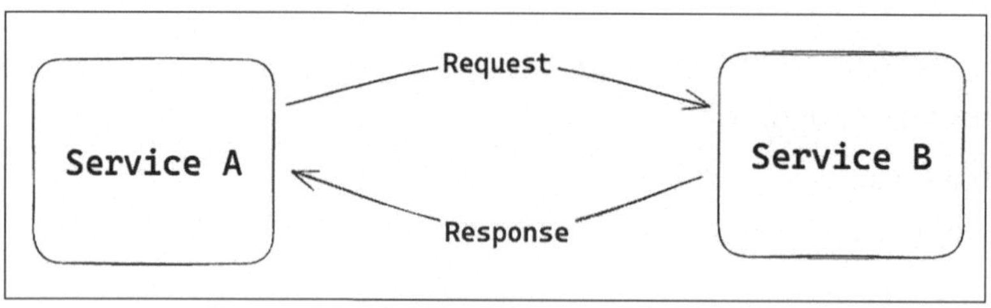

Figure 6.1: *API Call*

Message Brokers

We mentioned message brokers in the previous chapter and compared them to the Pub/Sub design pattern. A fitting description for message brokers is to characterize them as an intermediary of messages between one service and another. Instead of sending a request directly from one service to another, a service sends a message to a broker. The message contains mainly data, configuration, and sometimes instructions. The message broker is a separate service, often composing many services and acting as an independent cluster. The broker's goal is to receive the message and notify another service/s about this message or store it until another service pulls it. Message brokers have many additional capabilities like retries, store DLQ (aka for Dead Letter Queue), monitoring, temporary storage, encryption, controlling the pace of message mediation, and so on.

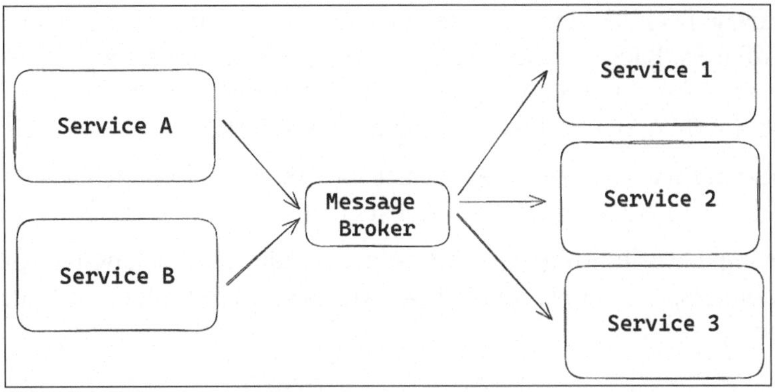

Figure 6.2: *Message Broker*

It is important to emphasize that building a message broker from scratch is strenuous and not recommended. There are various excellent and well-tested technologies in the market. Here are the leading ones:

- Apache Kafka
- RabbitMQ
- Amazon MQ

gRPC

gRPC is a modern, open-source Google Remote Procedure Call (RPC) **framework**. gRPC allows language-agnostic API definitions to be defined using Protocol Buffers. Protocol Buffers (protobuf) is a language-agnostic serialization format that is efficient for structuring and serializing data. We can quickly create client and server implementations using Protocol Buffers in various programming languages. gRPC framework leverages HTTP/2 as the underlying protocol, allowing multiple capabilities like bidirectional streaming and real-time communications. Behind the scenes, it is just an API call, but it takes advantage of HTTP/2 capabilities, which makes it very powerful. While simple APIs are straightforward, gRPC takes little time to learn. Moreover, the gRPC framework doesn't have support for all programming languages.

API Gateway

There are various ways to communicate between services in a microservices architecture. The standard way is via simple APIs, as we saw.

API gateway is a service that acts as an entrance (gateway) to the microservice architecture. The API gateway accepts all the requests from all the clients and then directs the client request to the desired service, also returns the response to the client. Having a single entrance point to the system gives us complete **control** over what is going in and out. We can implement a few capabilities categories using the API gateway:

- **Security**: Each service can use authentication, authorization, and encryption capabilities. Each service doesn't have to force those security requirements. Instead, most things can happen in the API gateway. Sometimes, it isn't feasible to do anything due to business logic constraints.
- **Observability**: Each service Can use capabilities like metrics, logs, and traces. We can start tracking all the requests from the API Gateway.
- **Routing**: Rate-limiting, caching, failure handle, load balancing, rolling updates capabilities, and more. All of those logics can be implemented inside the API gateway.

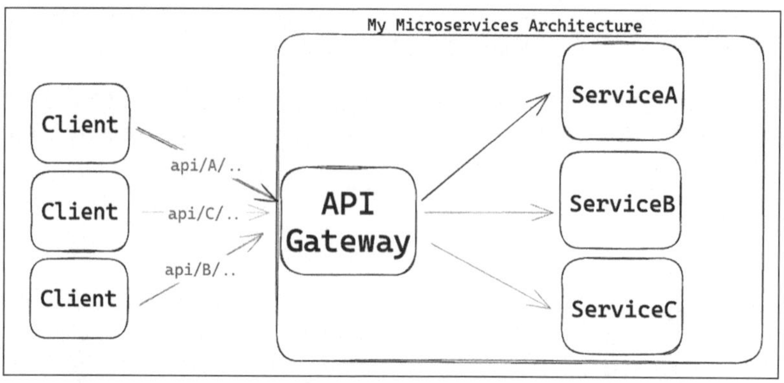

Figure 6.3: API *gateway, clients sending requests to services*

In the preceding figure, we can see different clients sending requests to the API gateway. The API knows how to direct each request to the desired service by the requested path and domain. This example illustrates the API gateway routing capability, among others we mentioned.

The most crucial thing to remember while building architecture is prioritizing **simplicity**. The API gateway pattern is beneficial and powerful because it helps us achieve simpler architecture. It centralizes many worries - security, observability, load balancing, rate-limit, and so on. When a problem occurs, we'll know where to investigate the incident.

Note that each API gateway varies from one to another. Each architecture has different requirements, leading to different API gateway approaches. *Chapter 8, Introduction to Kubernetes*, will discuss how Kubernetes independently implements some API gateway pattern capabilities - using a resource called ingress.

Service Discovery

In a microservices architecture, the way for services to communicate between them, as we said, is through APIs. Whenever a service needs to send an API request, it must determine the targeted service's network location (IP address and port). Each service may have several instances due to system requirements (each server has limitations to how many requests he can handle concurrently). Each service instance has a different network location (IP address and port). In the dynamic cloud environment, the network location of each service instance is temporary and changing urgently due to updates, scaling, failures, and so on. We need assistance identifying the existing service instances and their corresponding network locations.

The solution for this problem is the service discovery. The service discovery pattern lets a service know the network location of the requested service instance. The requested service can start communicating with the desired service when he learns the service network location. There are two patterns for implementing service discovery, as follows:

- Client-side discovery
- Server-side discovery

Client-Side Discovery

The client determines the requested service's instance network location using this pattern. The requesting service sends a request to a known storage that keeps each service's network locations. The so-called **service registry** is the storage that owns the network locations of all service instances.

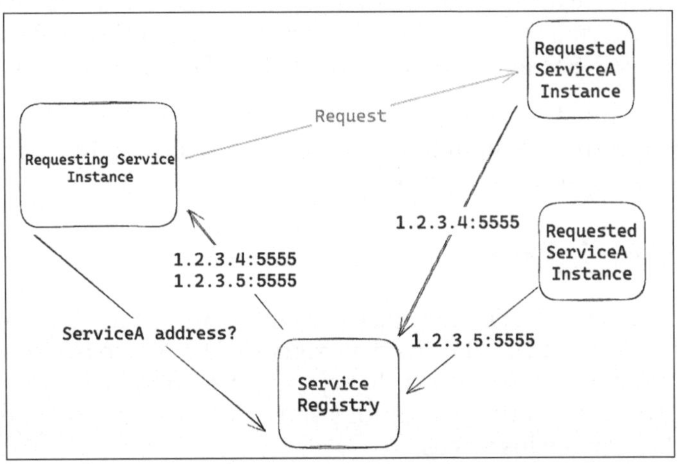

Figure 6.4: *Service discovery via client-side discovery*

The **Requesting Service Instance** asks the service registry for the network locations of **ServiceA** instances via the HTTP request. The service registry has the network locations of the **ServiceA** instance. The service instances are responsible for sending their network locations to the service registry. After the **Requesting Service Instance** gets the network location, he can request every **ServiceA** instance he wishes. In the preceding figure, we request the instance with the address **1.2.3.4:5555**.

The main drawback of this pattern is that we must implement a complex logic of load balancing and discovery logic on the client side, which means that we must duplicate the logic for each programming language.

Server-Side Discovery

This Server-Side Discovery pattern is the more prevalent of the two. In this pattern, all the "*problems*" are transferred to a load balancer, which counts as the "*Server*." The client sends a request to the load balancer, and the load balancer acts like the client in the client-side discovery pattern.

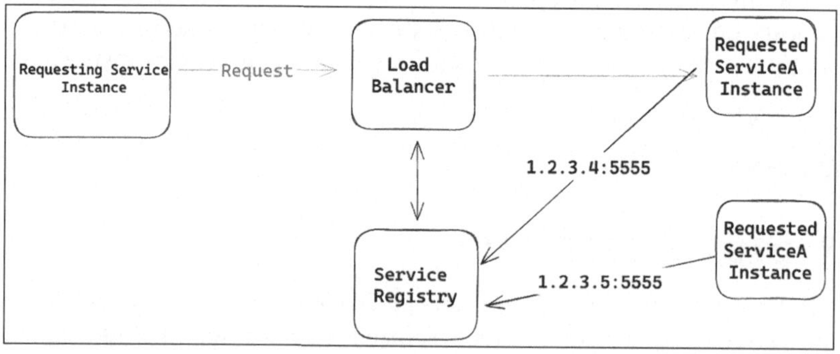

Figure 6.5: *Service discovery via server-side discovery*

All the functionality regarding load balancing is in the **`Load Balancer`** instead of the client. This pattern separates the discovery logic from the **`Requesting Service Instance`** to the **`Load Balancer`**, which is the main advantage of this pattern.

NGINX, AWS ALB, and AWS ELB are popular load balancers that can act as server-side. In *Chapter 8, Introduction to Kubernetes*, we will discuss Kubernetes, which has implemented a service discovery pattern using the server-side approach.

Service Registry

We already mentioned the service registry components while discussing client-side and server-side approaches. The service registry is a database containing all the service instances' network locations. It exposes the ability of service instances to register/unregister their network locations and delegates the job of network location registration to the service instances.

Moreover, the service registry requires them to send their heartbeat to determine if instances are still alive and can accept traffic. As we can see, there isn't an explicit service registry in Kubernetes; instead, Kubernetes leverages existing storage - etcd. Kubernetes has an internal logic that registers instances' network locations to etcd. Etcd is used for that purpose and has many other usages by Kubetenes. Etcd, in general, is a highly available, distributed, consistent key-value storage.

Load Balancer

A load balancer is a crucial component of any software architecture. On the one hand, we have various clients who wish to request a service from our system. On the other side, our dynamic and changing environment composes our services. Our environment can be highly dynamic due to version updates, failures, load, and many reasons. Between those two sides stands the load balancer, a policeman who routes the traffic.

The load balancer is responsible for regulating and distributing the network traffic among the existing servers and doing it effectively. It should know which services are currently available and which aren't. Understanding the services' availability can direct new requests and redirect existing requests from a faulty service to an operating service. It ensures the availability and reliability of all services.

As mentioned, the service discovery server can act as a load balancer, and the API gateway can serve as the service discovery. Therefore, the API gateway can be a load balancer. When talking about load balancers, the primary intention is the ability to distribute requests to available services. Request distribution can be highly complex, and we will give examples of different use cases and algorithms in a second.

There are various types of load balancers. This section of the book mainly describes L7 load balancers. A trendy way to divide different groups of load balancers is by L4 and L7. L4 load balancers are for the transport layer and focus on network layers like IP addresses and ports, while L7 load balancers concentrate on the application layer. Nowadays, there is no need to write a load balancer. Various load balancers, such as NGINX, HAProxy, AWS ELB, and AWS ALB exist.

This expansive subject could also fill an entire book with discussion. It is important to emphasize that load balancers are **necessary** and, luckily, easy to operate (usually). Unless we wish to write a load balancer or contribute to an existing project, we should focus on knowing only how to deploy, troubleshoot, and use it. The usage and configuration vary from one load balancer to another, and we can usually find an online guide that will walk us through how to deploy it.

The next point to understand is the algorithm governing the load balancer. We can configure a load balancer to our specific needs and requirements. Each load balancer technology has a variety of algorithms. Eventually, selecting the appropriate load balancer algorithm is essential for meeting our system requirements. Here are some widely used algorithms for load balancing:

- **Round Robin:** The request is distributed sequentially, one after another, in a loop. Round Robin is the most common and straightforward algorithm.
- **Least Connections:** The server with the lowest number of connections gets the next request.
- **Least Time:** A formula that calculates a combination of the number of connections and response time; the server that is faster and has a lower number of connections gets the next request.
- **Hash:** A key definition for distributing the request. The key definition can be the URL path, encoding type, port, IP address, and so on.

- **Random with Two Choices:** Choose two servers using an algorithm (Least Connections, Least Time, or something else), and select one randomly.

There are benefits and drawbacks to every algorithm. When choosing a load balancer algorithm, we should investigate and seek the best algorithm that suits our system. Other configurations can also benefit our system.

Database per Service

Database per service is a typical pattern in microservice architecture. Every system with multiple services will likely need a persistent data storage system. Establishing robust data separation is paramount in fostering loose coupling among services within a microservices architecture. Keep in mind that different services have different data storage requirements. Rational databases will be a great option; sometimes, NoSQL and others are the best. But that isn't the focus here.

Data separation can occur internally in the database itself – the so-called shared database pattern. However, in this pattern, we'll discuss the database per service. Let's illustrate the difference between a shared database (rational database, for example) and a database per service in a microservices architecture.

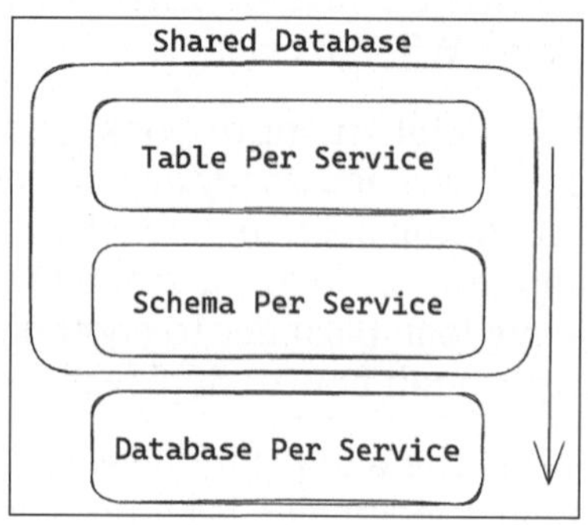

Figure 6.6: *Shared database in the rational database vs. database per service*

A shared database among various services can be through a single database and table or schema per service. Developers are often tempted to perform SQL joins or read another service data directory. To avoid this temptation, we can use the Database per Service pattern. The separation of databases per service gives us the highest level of separation, which manifests itself in several advantages:

- The services are loosely coupled - as we want!
- Each service can use a different database. As we mentioned, each database has other needs.
- Scaling limitation - many databases have limitations in terms of speed and size. When we have a separation of databases per service, it is easier to replicate and scale. We can manage each database independently, free from constraints imposed by other services.

However, separating databases per service has a few disadvantages:

- The complexity significantly increases when creating and managing more databases.
- Aggregations and joins between services become much more complicated and challenging. SQL joins are between different databases. Therefore, we need an external service or tool to facilitate it.
- Implementing transactions across services becomes tricky and complex. Distributed transactions are challenging; however, using the Saga pattern mentioned earlier might help us resolve it.

Imagine the pattern of database per service as another barrier between the services. Many companies usually use a shared database at the start because it is easy and fast. After a while, they realize they must separate the database per services/s. Still, the time-spending cost of separating the databases after a long time is very high compared to the scenario in which they would first separate a database per service.

Backends for Frontends

BFF, or Backends for Frontends, is a pattern that helps us improve client communication with our backend system. When building a system, we usually have different types of clients: web-based applications using HTML/JS, web frameworks like React, mobile clients for iOS or Android, desktop applications, direct API requests, or third-party applications. Each client will need data from a different variety of backend services in a different structure.

Our problem is how all those clients can communicate with all the backend servers without overcalling the complexity and making it cumbersome. The solution is to use the API gateway pattern discussed earlier in this chapter but for each client.

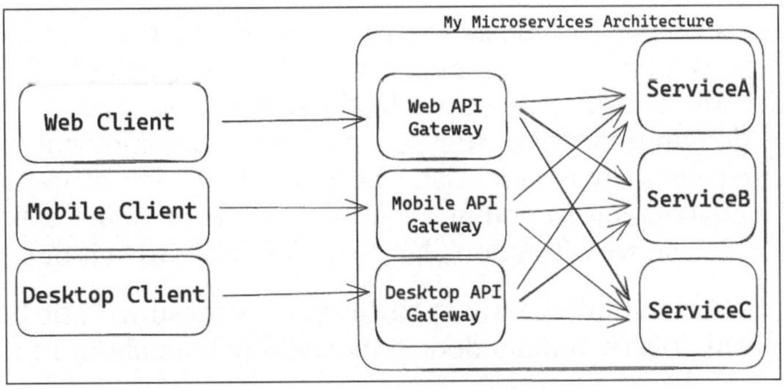

Figure 6.7: *Backends for frontends through API gateways*

This pattern's main disadvantage is the same disadvantage of the API gateway we described: the need to maintain another service, another moving part, which adds complexity. Also, adding another service is another network hop that causes slower latency.

On the other hand, using backends for frontends has the same advantages as API gateway. Backends for Frontends pattern is beneficial when creating optimal APIs for each client. The optimization of each client can vary from one client to another; for example, web-based applications probably need much more data than mobile applications.

External Configuration

While developing services in microservices architecture, we deploy the code we write into several environments, not one. Every environment is isolated from one another. The popular environment types are production, staging (sometimes called pre-production), QA, and development. Each service will need a different configuration in each environment. For example, each environment has a separate DB, connection configurations to third-party services are diverse, credentials, and many other differences. We don't want to create a duplication of each service; as developers, we hate duplications (DRY). The problem is deploying all those services to different environments without creating code duplications.

The solution is this pattern – make the configuration external to the service. When the service starts, it will pull a configuration from an external service/source via environment variables most of the time. Configuration injection can also be performed in other ways than environment variables. It is essential to be cautious. Confusion between environment configurations can be very painful, like switching the DB configuration of dev and production.

In *Chapter 8, Introduction to Kubernetes*, we will see how Kubernetes seamlessly helps in injecting configuration through the environment variables. A widespread tool, Helm, is a force multiplier above Kubernetes and provides a templating engine for even more seamless configuration.

Service Mesh

The best way to describe service mesh is as a dedicated infrastructure layer that handles communication between microservices. It usually provides tools in the network layer like elements described in this chapter - load balancers, service discovery, security, and monitoring (logging, metrics, and so on). Understanding that this technology exists and can help us a lot is essential. The main drawback of using service mesh is that it can be challenging to configure. When we reach some capability that our framework doesn't exist, we often don't have the flexibility to suit our needs.

Three popular market technologies that provide service mesh are Istio (for Kubernetes), Linkerd, and Consul. It is recommended to thoroughly read about it; this section was just a summary.

Event-Driven Architecture

Event-driven architecture is a vast topic. We'll discuss the collision of implementing event-driven architecture with microservices architecture. Event-driven architecture is a fascinating topic, and unfortunately, we won't be able to discuss it properly in this book. Instead, a highly recommended book for this topic is "*Designing Event-Driven Systems*".

Before jumping into the interface of microservices with event-driven, let's understand the basics of event-driven architecture.

Event Versus Message

A **message** is specific, and we send a message from a particular service to another. Both services, the sender and the receiver, are aware of the schema. The sender requests data, and he knows how to request it from the receiver (by the agreed schema). On the other hand, the receiver is expecting a request by the agreed schema by responding to the data as promised. The schema is unique for the sender and receiver, and the location is pre-determined.

An **event** is something more general. An event will contain data, not requests or instructions. An event has no specific destination. It is emitted and broadcast to those who will listen and consume this event. The event also contains an ID to be unique. Events are immutable, and they can't be changed.

Event-driven architecture is based on the Pub/Sub pattern we learned in the previous chapters. We need three components to implement the event-driven architecture: publisher, event broker, and consumer, as discussed in the Pub/Sub pattern. Here are common usages of event-driven architecture:

- **Tracking another system's events**: If we want to create a system that tracks another system with events, we will probably be forced to build event-driven architecture.
- **Auditing**.
- **Big Data processing**: The CRUD operation can create many collisions; moving to event-driven architecture can reduce that friction.
- **Backend processing**: Due to requirements of business logic.

Pros

- **Decoupled Services**: Like microservices, event-driven architecture helps us even more to reduce the friction between services and turn them into loosely coupled.
- **Scalability**: For the same reason, Pub/Sub helps us scale. We can control the producer and consumers separately, scale them separately, handle failures, deploy new versions, and more.

Cons

- **Data consistency**: The downside of segregating publishers and subscribers is that subscribers may experience delays in processing events, mainly when dealing with a high volume of messages. Maintaining consistency and processing events becomes challenging, especially when events involve logic correlated with others or interactions with third-party services.

- **Duplicate events**: Event-driven architecture works with breakpoints. If something terrible happens, we can always "*redrive*" events from the previous checkpoint. The problem is that we may already have processed some events until the failure, so we must process the same events again.
- **Complexity**: As mentioned a few times in this book - our system will become more complex when we add more components and services.

Event Sourcing

Event sourcing is a pattern that helps to leverage the benefits and characteristics of events. Due to the power of the events, we don't have to expose **`update`** and **`delete`** operations. Instead, all the events will always be saved and aggregated when requested by a service. This is basically what event sourcing patterns do. Typically, services that use the API would like to perform CRUD (create, read, update, delete) operations on the data. Instead, the data would look like an aggregation of events into a state. The final result should be the same whether or not it is used in event sourcing.

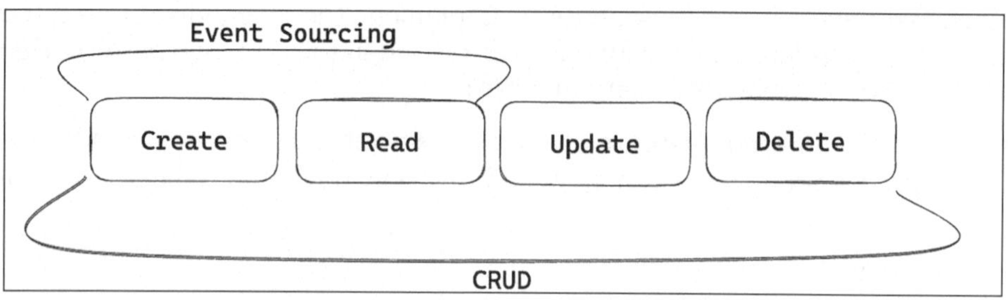

Figure 6.8: *Event sourcing vs. CRUD operations.*

Event sourcing "*shrinks*" the amount of CRUD operations. It "*disables*" the Update and Delete operation, "*enables*" only Create operation, and creates an alternative for the Read operation. This pattern has two advantages, including:

- **Immutability**: Everything is retained and updated. The original data is being saved, and we don't have to guess what the original data was. We get powerful visibility without significant effort of what exactly happened.
- **Replayability**: Bugs and problems will occur, eventually. In other scenarios, we had nothing to do with that. But now, we have all the data (events) needed to stream the event from when the bug was introduced.

The significant disadvantage of this pattern is that now we need to store much more data! Handling a large amount of data reveals many hidden problems. For example, we'll have to manage data retention, indexing, and integrity; this is just the tip of the iceberg. We can achieve data retention only when we know that we don't need those events at some point.

Instead, the querying time can be prolonged because we need to perform aggregation in each request, but for that, we have CQRS.

CQRS

CQRS, which stands for Command and Query Responsibility Segregation, is a pattern that helps us perform updates and reads in independent processes. CQRS is based on an event sourcing pattern. CQRS pattern aims to create a segregation between writing and reading handlers. As we mentioned, the user eventually wants to retrieve data, but the data is saved as a group of events. Instead of calculating the aggregation on each read request, each time an event is handled (creation), it triggers an aggregation of all the events with some logic. Finally, it will save the aggregation as a state into a view. A handler will expose an API to read the data from the view.

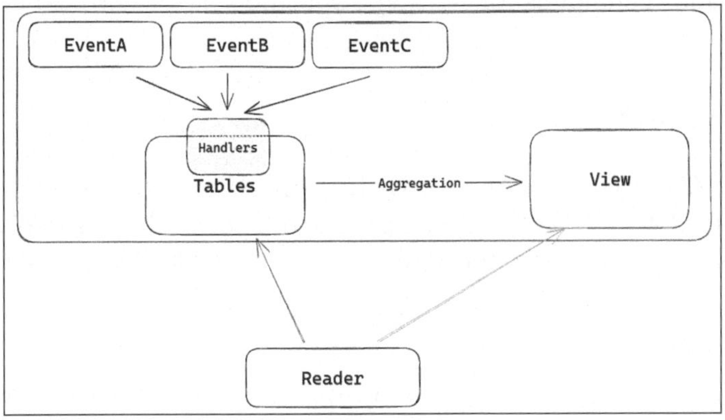

Figure 6.9: *CQRS standard usage*

The preceding figure shows three types of events - **`EventA`**, **`EventB`**, and **`EventC`**. All those event types are streaming events into the handlers (there is a Pub/Sub between them that we didn't draw). Then, the handlers write all the events into the **`Tables`**. Each write triggers a logic that calculates a state and writes that state into the **`View`**. When the user in the figure **`(Reader)`** wishes to read the data, it requests the **`View`** (green arrow) and not the **`Tables`** (red arrow).

The great advantage of CQRS is obvious - it gives us a fast read! Although the great advantage, there are two drawbacks to CQRS:

- We need to reduce all the events into a state, which sometimes can be a lot of data and consequently taking a long time to execute.
- The read is not available immediately after the write.

Conclusion

In this chapter, we briefly introduce the core elements of microservices architecture. Although we didn't delve into each element and pattern, we got a clear, bounded understanding of the significant elements of microservices architecture. Often, we won't use all the elements we described in this chapter in each microservices architecture. However, most of the patterns described in this chapter are implemented in various ways in most microservices architectures. Also, remember that we are developers, and the operations person (usually DevOps) will probably craft all those elements. They will set up all the necessary infrastructure to deploy our applications and services into production. As developers, we must understand how the entire system's operations work. This knowledge will assist us in understanding the boundary between our singular service to other services and the whole system.

All the elements we described don't include the business logic of our business. The business logic influences the decisions and designs of the elements discussed in this chapter. We didn't delve into the practices of writing a single service, which is the business logic. This is what we need to do in the next chapter. We will delve into the best practices and techniques for writing a specific service with Go in microservices architecture.

References

- https://www.thegeekyminds.com/post/how-microservices-communicate#:~:text=Message%20Brokers%20%2D%20Software%20tools%20called,an%20intermediate%20between%20various%20systems
- https://www.nginx.com/blog/service-discovery-in-a-microservices-architecture/
- https://www.nginx.com/learn/api-gateway/#:~:text=An%20API%20gateway%20is%20a%20data%2Dplane%20entry%20point%20for,%2C%20routing%2C%20and%20load%20balancing
- https://www.nginx.com/resources/glossary/load-balancing/
- https://medium.com/@crazy_nuclei/l4-vs-l7-load-balancers-64e47610e2ef#:~:text=In%20summary%2C%20L4%20load%20balancers,based%20on%20application%2Dspecific%20data
- https://hasithas.medium.com/introduction-to-message-brokers-c4177d2a9fe3
- https://pkg.go.dev/github.com/golang/protobuf
- https://microservices.io/patterns/data/database-per-service.html
- https://istio.io/
- https://linkerd.io/
- https://www.consul.io/

CHAPTER 7
Building RESTful API

Introduction

REST, which stands for REpresentational State Transfer, is an architectural style. REST defines sets of constraints that API should fulfill to meet the requirements of the REST style. RESTful is an adjective for an API that is ahead of REST constraints. In this first section of this chapter, we'll elaborate on these constraints.

In this chapter, we'll delve into the constraints of REST and illustrate them through a service in Go. In the previous chapter, we discussed the manner of communication between services in a microservices architecture. The prevalent pattern for communication is through API calls, with REST being the most widely adopted architectural style for APIs. Consequently, our primary focus will be on the REST architectural pattern. The microservices architecture inherently encompasses the REST constraints throughout the system and vice versa. There is a powerful connection between microservices and REST. More widely, there is an even more powerful connection between Microservices <> Go <> REST <> Kubernetes.

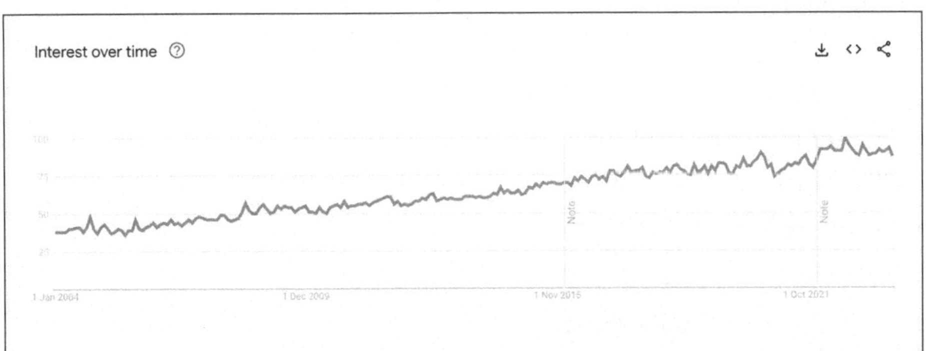

***Figure 7.1:** "REST" search term by Google Trends*

The REST approach has become very popular over the years, as we can see by Google Trends. With that popularity, many RESTful APIs exist, some of which became very popular due to their praiseworthy REST implementation. When learning REST at the start or just writing a new RESTful API, looking at famous APIs is pleasant and instructive. Here is an example of two of them:

- Strip API
- Twilio API

There are three topics that we won't cover in this chapter and will cover in the next chapters that are related to REST:

- Design of Failures
- Monitoring
- Security - Authentication, Authorization

It is vital to remember that REST is an architectural style, and there isn't a single way or the right way to implement REST. Some things are suitable for REST, and some are apparent and opposed to REST. In any meeting room, when designing REST APIs, there will be the stricter REST people called RESTafarians, and there are people who can deviate from REST's hard constraints. We sometimes can deviate from the constraints of REST to simplify/improve the API or answer edge cases. REST style is not boolean, 1, or 0. It is more abstract, and API can be "*more* REST" or "*less* REST".

Structure

In this chapter, we will discuss the following topics:

- A Brief About the RESTful Approach
    - Resource and Representation
    - Constraints
- Designing an API
    - Capabilities
    - Documentation - Swagger and OpenAPI
    - API Folder Structure
    - Resources Methods
- Crafting a Server
    - Gin Gonic Setup
    - Chains of Responsibilities
    - CORS
- API Capabilities
    - Pagination
    - Rate Limit
    - Panic Recovery
    - Graceful Shutdown

- Filter and Sort
- Caching
- Conventions
- Versioning and Deprecation
- Common Pitfalls

A Brief About the RESTful Approach

As we mentioned in the introduction, REST is a set of constraints, and RESTful API is an API that meets the constraints of REST. Let's emphasize that REST is a style, not a Protocol like HTTP. There is a familiar mix-up between REST and HTTP. Roy Fielding allows the use of any preferred protocol to implement REST. Although this option is available, most RESTful APIs use HTTP protocol, which Roy recommended as the preferred protocol, but it isn't a mandate. Other types of protocols can be FTP, SMTP, IMAP, and so on. The popular type of representation (the RE from REST) is JSON (stands for JavaScript Object Notation), and again, this isn't a constraint. RESTful API can use other representations like XML, HTML, CSV, plain text, PDF, and so on.

There are various ways to craft a RESTful API, depending on our choices, needs, and business constraints. Eventually, every RESTful API fulfills the REST constraints, but in different ways.

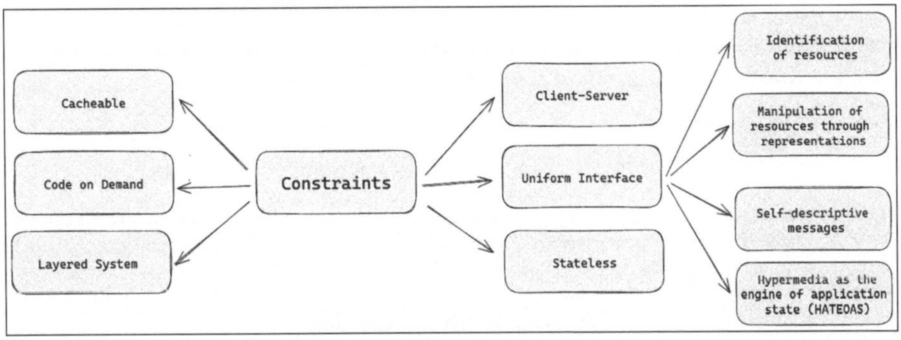

Figure 7.2: *REST constraints*

There are six constraints of REST. Eventually, we can do whatever we want with our code. The REST style aims to guide us in building a more sensible system. Implementing these constraints aims to improve the client's performance, stability, and scalability on the server side. These constraints are combined to solve and fix common and familiar problems that most systems have already experienced and been burned by.

Resource and Representation

We have mentioned resources and representation a few times. These two terms are the core of the REST style.

- **Resource:** A resource is a piece of information representing functional data as a single unit. For example, resources can be an object (account, user, chair), collection of objects, document, picture, and so on. We can change the state of resources by using so-called resource methods, which need to be uniform (as the Uniform Interface constraint). For example, HTTP methods like GET, POST, PUT, DELETE, and more behave as the resource methods.
- **Representation:** Resource representation refers to the state of the resource, which includes data, metadata, and hyperlinks.

Constraints

Here are the six constraints.

Client-Server

This constraint is also the core principle of microservices architecture. It encourages us to keep client and server loosely coupled. The client and the server must not share any dependency between them. Components need to be developed independently and separately; the client only knows the URIs that the server exposes.

Uniform Interface

This is the most complex constraint, composed of four other sub-constraints. URI, which stands for Uniform Resource Identifier, is a sequence of characters web technologies know to recognize and associate specific resources.

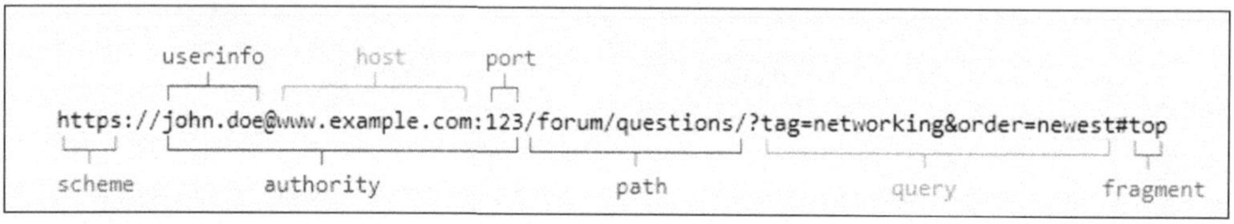

Figure 7.3: *URI composition*

Unlike the protocol and representation mentioned earlier, URIs aren't a choice. REST forces us to use URIs to determine the uniqueness of resources. Between the server and the client, there is an interface. This constraint aims to create solidarity while establishing that interface by the four sub-constraints:

- **Identification of resources:** It involves ensuring that each URI is unique to a specific resource. This uniqueness is crucial, preventing the manipulation of the same resource from different interfaces.
- **Manipulation of resources through representations:** The representation the server needs to expose is the desired modification. This representation needs to be as explicit as possible.

For example, the HTTP method like DELETE + URI to a specific resource (**`DELETE https://domain:port/api/account/{accountId}`**) indicates that the client requests the API to delete an account that has **`accoundId`** Account ID. The developer must understand the URI easily without further documentation (at least most of the time).

- **Self-descriptive messages:** The message must contain all the "*instructions*" on the desired resource. The server should only have all the necessary information from the message without further questions or information.
- **Hypermedia As The Engine Of Application State (HATEOAS) :** Hypermedia refers to all forms of media such as movies, pictures, files, and more. When a client requests the RESTful API server to get data on a resource, it expects to get that resource's data. A portion of the data can be hypermedia, and REST aims to provide links to the media data instead of the data in some form.

Stateless

Each request from the client to the server is isolated. The server must neither rely on previous requests in any manner nor on the local dynamic context of the server. Client requests must contain all the necessary data to execute the request as desired.

Layered System

Each request from the client to the server goes through layers. There is never a direct connection between the client and the business logic. These layers can be, for example, authentication, caching, load balancing, and more. This constraint encourages us to create separated layers between the client and the server, such as in microservices architecture. The client is agnostic to the different layers between him and the server. Most layers often exist in the API gateway – as described in the previous chapter.

Cacheable

This constraint forces the server to return a response, which includes data indicating whether the data is from the cache.

Code on Demand

This constraint isn't frequent nor required. The server can provide the client with additional functionality by downloading applets or scripts. For example, the client wants to convert JPEG to PDF, so he requests from the server a script that does it. The client gets the script and executes it.

Designing an API

Before approaching writing a service, the first step is to understand the product requirements, engineering constraints, and anything that can impact decisions.

Define what it will look like, what the necessary capabilities are, what isn't, and how to implement it. Decide what the available resources are and their corresponding representations.

Capabilities

Standard capabilities across RESTful APIs are as follows:

- Documentation
- Authentication and Authorization (can be at the API gateway layer)
- RBAC (can be at the API gateway layer)
- Pagination
- Rate limit
- Caching
- Filtering
- Sorting
- Monitoring and Observability
- Feature toggling
- Alerting
- Error handling
- Auto code-client generated

Each API probably doesn't need all those capabilities and probably needs other capabilities we didn't mention here. When building microservices architecture, each API will want to implement a portion or more of these capabilities, probably in the same shape as the other APIs. If we implement the same capabilities repeatedly for each API (even if we use a package for each capability), we will end up with tons of boilerplate code that differs slightly in each API.

To solve this problem, we need to create a shared infrastructure. One way to implement shared infrastructure is through shared code (when using monorepo). In Go, this code will be in a directory called `pkg`. Another way to implement shared infrastructure is to use SDKs (when using `polyrepo`); each API will import and use this SDK for its own needs).

Documentation: Swagger and OpenAPI

The most crucial part of constructing an API is documenting the API specification. An industry standard to document the API specification is to use Swagger and OpenAPI.

OpenAPI is the official name for a specification that standardizes API documentation. It has a unique syntax and can be written in JSON or YAML.

Swagger is a set of tools that helps implement OpenAPI. Most Swagger tools are accessible in the OSS project; paying is an option for advanced tools.

- **Swagger Editor**: A tool allowing us to edit Swagger YAML online and view the changes.
- **Swagger UI**: A tool that generates UI for OpenAPI specification.
- **Swagger Codegen**: With OpenAPI specific, Swagger Codegen can generate various API clients and servers in many programming languages.
- Other tools that can help with various needs that we will not mention here.

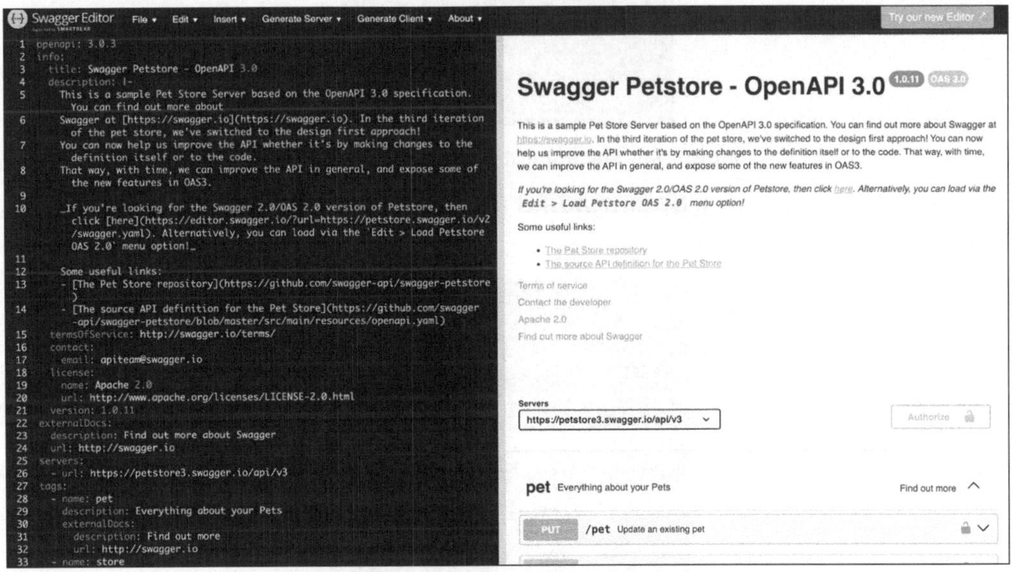

Figure 7.4: *Swagger editor (https://editor.swagger.io/)*

Swagger is the most potent and widespread set of tools due to its simple syntax, but it has many options for describing APIs. The agreement between the client and the server is to use centralized documentation. Many times, the developers/teams that work on the API server vary from the developers/teams that work on the client.

API Folder Structure

In *Chapter* 3, *Go Essentials*, we discussed Go's folder structure. We'll combine that folder structure with the API folder structure into a united structure. A well-designed folder structure will serve the developers' needs. From onboarding – whether they know the project or not – the navigation will be without hesitation until writing code – where to find logic and where to add new resources or capabilities.

Here, we'll show two famous file structures, but first, let's observe their commonalities.

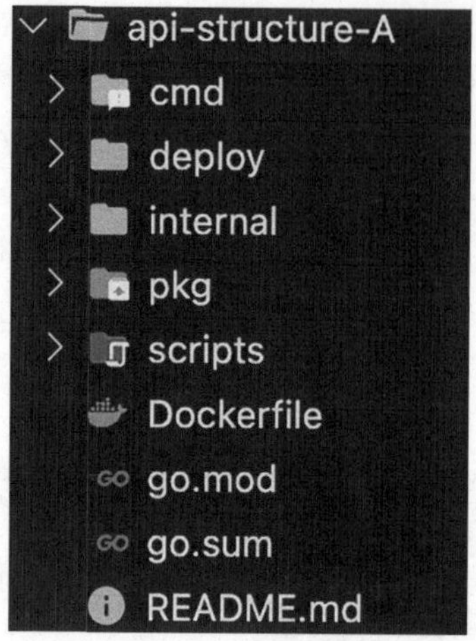

Figure 7.5: *The highest level of API structure*

The first folder is **`cmd`**, which we already discussed, but now we have another executable: the **`docs`**.

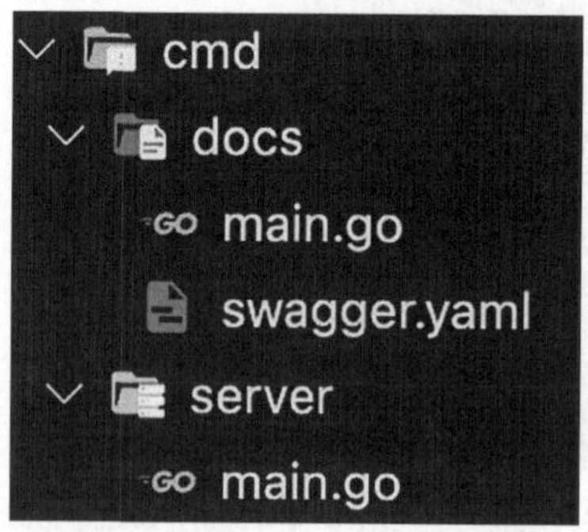

Figure 7.6: *cmd structure in API*

The **`docs`** directory contains another **`main.go`**, which is the entry point like the server **`main.go`** but for deploying the documentation. We can use Swagger UI to generate UI on the **`swagger.yaml`**.

The second directory name is **`deploy`**, which contains all the configurations for deploying the executables and other assets that are related to the server, such as networking, configuration, autoscaling, and more. The **`pkg`** and **`scripts`** directories have the same purpose as described in the third chapter - they contain shared code between servers and scripts, respectively. The files **`go.mod, go.sum, README.md,`** and **`Dockerfile`** will be in the leading directory.

In the two examples of API structures, we'll follow the structure of a grocery store. For simplicity, we'll divide the products in the shop into two categories (so-called tags in OpenAPI) - **fruits** and **vegetables**.

For the category of fruits, we have apples and bananas. For the category of vegetables, we have tomatoes and cucumbers. Each fruit (apple, banana) and each vegetable (tomato, cucumber) is a resource by the REST definition. We can buy more cucumbers (CREATE), see how many cucumbers we have (READ), sell some of them (DELETE), or update their new price today (UPDATE).

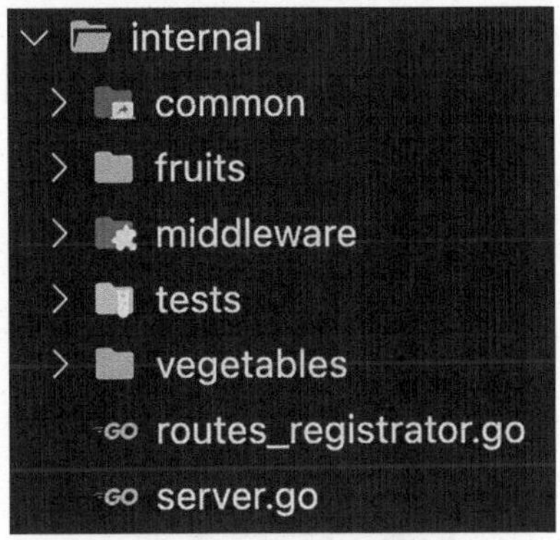

***Figure 7.7:** API internal file structure* A

The preceding figure presents the file structure for option A, which is the only difference between option B. Let's go through the directories and files inside it.

- **`common`**: This directory includes boilerplate code used across all resources, shared functionality, utils, and abstraction that each resource needs to use. For example, a file called **`query-params.go`** helps to serialize all query parameters from the request.
- **`middleware`**: The middleware fulfills the constraint of a layered system. In this directory, we'll find the layers. These layers exist between the request's entry point and the endpoint handler. Examples of middleware can be:
  - Authentication and authorization
  - Caching
  - Request parsing
  - Logging
  - Rate limit
  - Monitoring
  - Security
  - Caching
  - Adding context for business logic, such as connection to cache or database
- **`tests`**: Contains all the service tests. Here, we'll elaborate on the internal structure of the tests.
- **`routes_registrator.go`**: Each resource has several endpoints. This file aggregates all the routes and registers them to the API so the **`server.go`** will know to direct each request to the desired handler.

- **`server.go`**: Build the API engine. It uses the **`routes_registor.go`**, uses the middleware, and sets the portion of the configuration.
- **Directory for each category (tag)**: There is a different directory for each tag - fruits, vegetables, and so on.

Figure 7.8: *API structure option A for each category*

There is a different directory for each resource in each category directory. Note that a single resource can contain several endpoints. For example, **`GET /api/fruits/apple/:id, POST /api/fruits/apple, UPDATE /api/fruits/apple/:id, DELETE /api/fruits/apple/:id`** – all of these four endpoints are related to the same resource – apple. In each resource directory, there can be four files:

- **`controller.go`**: This is the primary handler where the request starts after all the middlewares. It parses the request, notifies the client of errors (4XX status code), and returns the data by the OpenAPI commitment.
- **`db.go:`** This is sometimes named as - **`repository.go`**. This file contains all the operations against the database, whichever database it is. The power of this structure is that we can switch databases, and all we need to take care of are the **`db.go`** files. Note that this file shouldn't contain the model/entity by itself. Usually, there is a separate mechanism for managing the database, like ORM and migrations tool (gorm is a standard and widely used tool for achieving ORM).
- **`routes.go:`** Define all the endpoints for a resource. Note that a single resource can contain several endpoints. This file will contain a function like this:

```
func RegisterRoutes(group *gin.RouterGroup) {
      group.GET("/fruits/apple/search",gin.HandlersChain{Process
RequestSearch}...)
group.GET("/fruits/apple/:id", gin.HandlersChain{ProcessRequestID}...)
}
```

- **`service.go`:** It contains all the business logic.

The second option for the file structure is similar. The main difference is in the order of the files and directories.

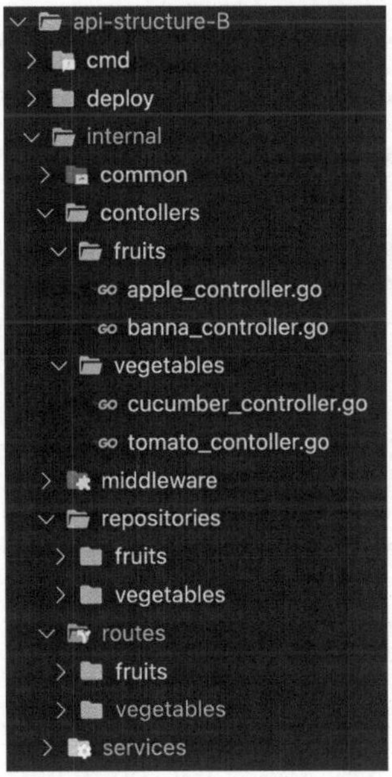

***Figure 7.9:** API structure option B*

We created four files for each resource in a single directory in the previous structure.

We are creating four directories in option B: **`controllers`**, **`routes`**, **`repositories`**, and **`services`**. In each directory, we'll find another group of directories as the number of categories and, in each one, a single file for each resource.

Resources Methods

As mentioned, REST doesn't force us to use specific protocols, but the HTTP method currently dominates the market as the most used REST protocol. This section will focus on HTTP; however, we can conduct the same behavior on other protocols.

- **`GET`**: It is used to retrieve information only; it doesn't change the state in any way. This method represents the Read operation. Each time we use the **`GET`** method, we should get the same result, unless another request by another

HTTP method modified the resource. Such types of requests can be cacheable and have length restrictions. Examples:

```
GET https://www.example.com/accounts
GET https://www.example.com/accounts/search?name=john
GET https://www.example.com/accounts?page=5
```

- **POST**: It creates new data for a particular resource – a single row or several rows. This type of request can't be cacheable and has no length restriction. Usually, data is sent in the request body and not in the URI. POST and GET methods are the most widely used over HTTP methods. Examples:

```
POST https://www.example.com/accounts
POST https://www.example.com/accounts/myaccount_id/users
```

- **PUT**: It is usually used to update an existing resource state. However, it can also create new data like the **POST** method. The main difference between **POST** and **PUT** is that **PUT** is idempotent, and **POST** isn't. This difference means that calling the **PUT** method several times will give the same result, while **POST** doesn't promise that due to potential side effects. Example:

```
PUT https://www.example.com/accounts/{myaccount_id}
```

- **DELETE**: It is used to delete specific resources.
- **Others**: **PATCH, OPTIONS, HEAD, CONNECT,** and **TRACE** are other HTTP methods we can use but aren't as often as the preceding methods.

Let's briefly overview the standard HTTP status codes (X refers to any number, and 1XX means 100-199):

- **1XX**: Information responses. They aren't used often.
- **2XX**: Successful responses, the status code we'll want to see.
  - 200 OK: Usually used by the **GET** method to determine that the data is retrieved successfully.
  - 201 Create: Usually used by **POST/PUT.**
- **3XX**: Redirection message, usually used to redirect requests to other servers, endpoints, domains, and so on.
- **4XX**: Client errors responses, meaning there is a problem with the request, which is the client's responsibility. These kinds of responses are caught in the middleware or the controller.
  - **400 Bad Request**: The client didn't give the correct/right information to process the request.
  - **401 Unauthorized**: The server can't identify the client.
  - **403 Forbidden**: The client is identified but cannot access the requested data.

  - **404 Not Found**: It is among the most popular status codes, indicating that the request is unrecognized.
- **5XX**: Server error responses, meaning a problem with the server himself, and the users usually don't have much to do with that.
  - **500 Internal server error**: The server went into a scenario we don't know how to handle.

Crafting a Server

This section will review the essentials of creating a RESTful API server in Go. We'll focus on setting up a server with Gin and what to notice. Go provide us with a default package called http, which we'll use and utilize.

Gin Gonic Setup

Gin is an HTTP web framework. First, we'll start from the **`main.go`**, where we declare and execute a server.

```
func main() {
	port := 8080
	engine := internal.BuildEngine()

	srv := &http.Server{
		Addr:    fmt.Sprintf(":%d", port),
		Handler: engine,
	}

	log.Printf("Starting server on port %d", port)
	if err := srv.ListenAndServe(); err != nil && err != http.Err-
	ServerClosed {
		log.Print("error while running API gin server", "error",
		err.Error())
		os.Exit(1)
	}
}
```

After declaring the port and building the gin engine (we'll see how in a second), we created an instance of **`http.Server`** struct. After that, we started the server using the **`ListenAndServe()`** function.

```
func BuildEngine() *gin.Engine {
	engine := gin.New()
	engine.Use(gin.Logger())
	engine.Use(gin.Recovery())
	engine.Use(CORS())
	group := engine.Group("/api")
	RegisterRoutes(group)
	// engine.use(<any middleware you want>)
	return engine
}
```

To create a new engine, we used **gin.New()**. While building the engine, we'll declare all the middlewares that apply to all endpoints in the server. In the example, these include logger, recovery, and CORS (we'll discuss them in the next section). After declaring all the wanted middlewares, we'll declare the groups. Gin let us divide the server into groups. We won't focus on it and assign a single group for all the servers. Sometimes, developers assign a group to a category and a subgroup to a subcategory. In the example, the group is just **"/api"**. We'll assign all the endpoints to the group by using the **RegisterRoutes** function in the **routes_registrator.go** file.

```
func RegisterRoutes(routerGroup *gin.RouterGroup) {
	apple.RegisterRoutes(routerGroup)
}
```

Using multiple groups in this function, we can assign more relevant middleware to that specific group. Now, let's observe the internal of a single endpoint is a single resource. This code is what we'll find in the **routes.go** file:

```
package apple


import "github.com/gin-gonic/gin"


var Path = "/fruits/apple"


func RegisterRoutes(group *gin.RouterGroup) {
	group.GET(Path, gin.HandlersChain{ProcessRequest}...)
}
```

And in the controller.go file:

```
package apple
```

```
import "github.com/gin-gonic/gin"

func ProcessRequest(c *gin.Context) {
	c.JSON(200, gin.H{
		"color": "red",
		"date":  "2023-12-11",
		"taste": "sweet",
	})
}
```

The response, of course, is just mocked data; instead, we'll need to execute a business logic function in the **server.go** file, which almost always will query the data from the **db.go** file.

Chains of Responsibilities

If we simplify it, chains of responsibility are a design pattern linking several commands so one command will lead to another. This pattern helps us fulfill the constraint of a layered system. The implementation of this pattern happens through middleware.

Using the modularity we presented before, we can apply relevant middleware to the entire API (in the **BuildEngine** function). We can be more specific and apply middleware to a particular group (a category) in the **RegisterRoutes** function. In even more detail, we can apply a particular middleware at the resource level in **routes.go**.

CORS

CORS, a browser security feature, stands for Cross-Origin Resource Sharing. This feature aims to restrict unwanted HTTP requests. We must specify what origins are acceptable for sending requests from a web browser to our RESTful API server. Here is how to create gin middleware that can take care of that:

```
func CORS() gin.HandlerFunc {
	return func(c *gin.Context) {
		c.Writer.Header().Set("Access-Control-Allow-Origin", "*")
		c.Writer.Header().Set("Access-Control-Allow-Credentials",
		"true")
		c.Writer.Header().Set("Access-Control-Allow-Methods",
		"POST, GET")
		c.Next()
	}
}
```

API Capabilities

As mentioned, each API needs to support capabilities that are derivatives of the product needs. Many popular capabilities exist in almost every API, and some are not. We'll elaborate here about the popular ones. Each API capability will probably be used by more than one API, at least the popular ones. The best practice is creating a configurable shared infrastructure that is served as a package or under the `pkg` directory if it is monorepo. For example, if one API uses a particular type of pagination, the other services in the same company will probably need to use pagination in the same manner.

Pagination

Pagination is the process of separating content into separate pages/parts. It is usually used for navigation or to get data if it is massive. For example, if a user reads an online book, we don't need to get all the book content simultaneously. Instead, we can ask for the next page whenever he swipes a page. Another example is when we need all the users of a specific account, but there is an enormous number of users, and it is impossible to get all of them as a single response; instead, we can use pagination.

There are various pagination algorithms, and a portion of the algorithm can be applied in the DB-level. For example, using limit and offset in SQL for PostgreSQL. The popular pagination algorithms are:

- **Page number:** The most straightforward and most unused algorithm. Choosing const limit, then multiply the limit and the page number.

  ```
  GET /api/users?page=2
  ```

- **Offset and Limit:** Like the previous pagination algorithm. The difference is that we must choose the limit size instead of the default limit. The client needs to use an offset between each request, which complies with the client interaction. This is the most used pagination algorithm.

  ```
  GET /api/users?limit=10
  GET /api/users?limit=10&offset=10
  GET /api/users?limit=10&offset=20
  ```

- **Auto Incremental PK of the ID:** Also a ubiquitous algorithm. This algorithm depends on some ID to arrange the data, and that ID is used as a cursor.

  ```
  GET /api/users?limit=10
  GET /api/users?limit=10&cursor=<last_id_from_previous_request>
  GET /api/users?limit=10&cursor=<last_id_from_previous_request>
  ```

Rate Limit

A rate limit is a way to block the over-using amount of users, bots, and requests. To keep the server up and functioning, we must limit the number of requests going to the server. The rate limit is usually a constant number of requests per interval, for example, 10,000 requests per minute.

We'll implement the rate limit as middleware in a shared package and use this middleware in every service. It is unnecessary to implement rate limits by ourselves. There are great packages that are suitable for gin to do so. Finally, the HTTP status code returned when the number of requests passed the limit of 429 (Too Many Requests).

Panic Recovery

We've already discussed error handling in Go and on **`panic()`** in a nutshell. We can liken panic to raise/throw exceptions in other programming languages. We use **`panic()`** when something unexpected happens, so we must crash the whole application. When writing RESTful API, the **`panic()`** inside an endpoint is odd because a single endpoint isn't supposed to affect other endpoints.

We must return the error status code if something terrible happened at that endpoint. When writing RESTful APIs, we'll probably **`panic()`** when the server goes up or functionality related to the whole server crashes. Please also note to use panic wisely because it will execute all the defer statements when a **`panic()`** occurs.

Developers often use **`panic()`** incorrectly and put it accidentally within an endpoint or use a package that propagates a **`panic()`** to our program. To tackle that scenario, we can create a middleware that can recover from panic. We can use the default panic recovery middleware of gin:

```
engine.Use(gin.Recovery())
```

Or we can craft custom panic recovery using the **`recover()`** function:

```
func WithCustomRecovery() gin.HandlerFunc {
	return func(c *gin.Context) {
		defer func() {
			if err := recover(); err != nil {
				_ = c.Error(fmt.Errorf("[recovered] panic: %v",
				err))
				c.AbortWithStatusJSON(http.StatusInternalS-
erverError, gin.H{"Error": "Internal Server Error"})
			}
		}()
```

```
		c.Next()
	}
}
```

In the preceding example, we crafted a custom recovery and can put any customized functionality we want. Not that this middleware will occur for each on-flight request.

Graceful Shutdown

Graceful shutdown is when a system or application is turned off or gets signals that it needs to go down (rollout or any other reason). While receiving a signal to go down, the application has on-flight tasks. Graceful shutdown gives the application a grace period to finish its tasks.

When building RESTful APIs, it is crucial to implement a graceful shutdown at the server level. We want to let all on-flight requests finish their work whenever something bad or a rollout occurs. Here is an example of a graceful shutdown from the **main.go**:

```
func main() {
	port := 8080
	engine := internal.BuildEngine()

	srv := &http.Server{
		Addr:    fmt.Sprintf(":%d", port),
		Handler: engine,
	}
	log.Printf("Starting server on port %d", port)

	startHTTPServer(srv)
}

func startHTTPServer(srv *http.Server) {
	// Create context that listens for the interrupt signal from the OS.
	sigCtx, stopSig := signal.NotifyContext(context.Background(),
syscall.SIGINT, syscall.SIGTERM)
	defer stopSig()

	go func() {
```

```
        if err := srv.ListenAndServe(); err != nil && err != http.
ErrServerClosed {
                log.Print("error while running API gin server", "er-
ror", err.Error())
                os.Exit(1)
        }
    }()

    // Listen for the interrupt signal.
    <-sigCtx.Done()
    // Restore default behavior on the interrupt signal and notify a
user of a shutdown.
    stopSig()

    // Requests are currently on-flight; wait 10 seconds for them to
    finish.
    ctx, cancel := context.WithTimeout(context.Background(), 10*time.
    Second)
    defer cancel()
    if err := srv.Shutdown(ctx); err != nil {
        log.Print("server forced to shutdown: ", "error", err.Error())
    }
}
```

The function that implements the graceful shutdown is **`startHTTPServer.`** First, we take the background context and listen for interrupted signals from the system. Then, we run the **`ListenAndServe()`** function in a goroutine. When some signal is received, we give the system 10 seconds to finish its work using **`context.WithTimeout`**. Note that this time is different between each server and depends on the server's internal functionality and the API purpose.

Filter and Sort

These two functionalities, filter and sort, are the most popular functionalities we can implement in an endpoint. This is in addition to the pagination functionality that we saw before.

Filter

There are three significant ways to implement filtering:

- **Path Parameters:** We've already mentioned path parameters in this chapter. Filtering by path parameter is usually used in specific use cases.

  ```
  GET /api/accounts/{category} -> GET /api/accounts/Enterprise
  ```

  In this example, we filtered all accounts from the Enterprise category. Of course, we'll need to declare it in the OpenAPI and implement it in the server.

- **Query Parameters:** These are the most popular way to perform filtering. The URL is supposed to be pretty straightforward, mainly using **'?'** and **'&'** keywords to separate between filtering parameters. Query parameters filtering has URL constraints, and we'll want to keep it as simple as possible. If it becomes more complicated, we should consider the third option for filtering.

  ```
  GET /api/accounts?category=Enterprise&size_gt=500
  ```

  In this example, we want to get all enterprise accounts whose size is greater than 500. On the same coin, we can use different filters like - **size_lt** (size it lower than), **size=** (size it is equal to), **size_not** (size isn't equal to), and **size_gte** (size is greater than or equal to).

- **Request Body:** Occasionally, we will need more complex filtering. Here, using body requests comes in handy.

  ```
  POST /api/accounts
  Content-Type: application/json

  {
      "or": {
          "category": "Enterprise",
          "size_gt": 500,
      }
  }
  ```

  In the preceding example, we used HTTP POST requests with JSON and asked for all the accounts that are enterprise or whose size is greater than 500.

Sort

Sorting is the ability of the API to arrange the responded data in a specific order, like the user requirements. There are three significant ways to sort data:

- **Ascending:** This technique is used to sort the data from the lowest value of a specific field to the highest value of the same field.

  ```
  GET /api/accounts?sort=size&order=asc
  ```

In the example, we sort all the accounts from a minor account to the biggest. The convention is to use the sort and order as query parameters.

- **Descending**: The same as ascending, but opposite. It returns the data from the highest value to the lowest value.

  ```
  GET /api/accounts?sort=size&order=desc
  ```

  The convention is to use asc for ascending and desc for descending.

- **Multiple Sorting:** When a single field is insufficient, we can use more complex sorting using multiple fields.

  ```
  GET /api/account?sort=effective_score,-size
  ```

  In the preceding example, the field **`effective_score`** is a rank number between 1 and 5 that determines how much to account for if effective. We want to retrieve the accounts from the most effective account (ascending order) with the smallest size (descending order due to - sign).

Caching

Caching is the ability to store data that is frequently used. The location of the cache can change depending on the situation. The place can be at the load balancer or server level, and distributed cache is usually an option using Redis. Let's have a quick reminder of HTTP methods caching:

- `GET`: Are cached by default unless a particular case occurs.
- `POST`: Aren't cached by default unless the request explicitly declares it wants cached data.
- `PUT and DELETE` aren't cachable at all.

To implement caching, we need to leverage the power of middleware and implement a middleware. The caching functionality relies upon TTL (Time-To-Live) and request header definitions:

- **Expires**: This header specifies the absolute time when the cache expires.

  ```
  Expires: Sun, 21 June 2023 16:27:59 GMT
  ```

- **Cache-Control**: This header declares directives, whether a response is cachable or not. Examples of directives are - **`max-age=3600, must-revalidate, no-cache`**, and so on. They can be found at https://developer.mozilla.org/en-US/docs/Web/HTTP/Headers/Cache-Control.
- **Last-Modified**: It determines when the last response was generated.

Lastly, it is essential to remember that the purpose of a cache is to improve latency and reduce server work while responding to the desired data. If the cache doesn't accomplish its original goal, we need to remove or fix the caching layer.

Conventions

Here, we will detail all the conventions and best practices related to RESTful API.

- A resource can be a collection or singleton. For example:

  `GET /api/accounts`: Collection resource

  `GET /api/accounts/{id}`: Singleton resource; when we wish to retrieve a singleton resource, we will use **`accounts`** in "*plural*".

- Collection/Singleton resource can contain sub-collection, for example:

  `GET /api/accounts/{id}/users - the users is the sub-collection resource.`

- **Use a noun, not a verb**: URI aims to describe a resource as an entity (noun) and not as an action (verb). Also, don't include the operation name in the URI.

  `GET /api/deleteAccounts/{id} - bad`

  `DELETE /api/accounts/{id} - good`

- **Chars convention**:
  - Use "-" to improve the readability of URI:

    `GET /api/user-management`

  - Don't use trailing flash:

    `GET /api/account/ - bad`

    `GET /api/account - good`

  - Always use forward slack '/' and not backward slash '\'
  - Avoid using file extension:

    `GET /api/accounts/billing.json - bad`

    `GET /api/accounts/billing - good`

In a few scenarios, the endpoint will become highly complicated, and we need to simplify it as much as possible. We should consider splitting it into two or more endpoints if it becomes overcomplicated.

Versioning and Deprecation

API is a commitment, and the documentation is a promise to the user. Developers want to introduce new features or make breaking changes due to product/engineering needs. Versioning the API comes in handy for achieving this goal. Versioning allows developers to make a clear separation between one promise and another (promise=version) without breaking existing clients.

Versioning Strategies

Let's take a look at the prevalent strategies for versioning the API.

- **URI Versioning:** The API version is included inside each endpoint.

  ```
  GET /api/v1/accounts
  GET /api/v2/accounts
  ```

  This method is trendy and very easy to implement. However, the REST approach desires to include only the resource details in the URI, not the version.

- **Query Parameter Versioning:** Like URI versioning, the version in the URI, but not as path parameter; instead, it is included as a query parameter.

  ```
  GET /api/account?version=1
  GET /api/account?version=2
  ```

  It is the same as the previous, less famous strategy but doesn't require the client to change the URL, only the parameter.

- **Header Versioning:** It includes a header that indicates the API version.

  ```
  GET /api/accounts
  Headers:  { "X-API-version": "1" }


  GET /api/accounts
  Headers:  { "X-API-version": "2" }
  ```

  This approach is most suitable with the REST approach. However, the version can be hidden from the user.

Versioning Best Practices

Let's explore some best practices:

- **Utilize three-part versioning**: The best practice for the versioning schema is as follows: **`major.minor.patch`**. For example, 1.3.2 - version major is 1, minor is 3, and patch is 2:
  - Major: To introduce breaking or massive API changes.
  - Minor: Every time new capabilities and features that are still backward-compatible are introduced,
  - Patch - bug fixes.
- **Backward compatibility**: Always aim to support old features and capabilities rather than break them. We use backward compatibility to reduce the effect on the end client.

- **Communicate Changes**: Whenever we release a new version, it is essential to reflect and elaborate on what was changed to the customer and to do it well.

Deprecation

We'll do it gracefully when it is necessary to deprecate old API versions. The grace period must be very long, and we must frequently report changes to the customers. We must give the users enough time to migrate to the new version. The documentation also reflects the deprecation, and endpoints are marked as deprecated.

Common Pitfalls

Here are some common pitfalls in REST:

- **Overusing POST HTTP method**: Developers tend to stick to POST operation even when it isn't the right choice. We must utilize all the other HTTP methods: `DELETE`, `PATCH`, `PUT`, `GET`, and so on.
- **Not sticking to a convention mentioned earlier:** The term resource can be confusing for REST newcomers, leading to lousy resource naming.
- **Lack of versioning**: We must keep the API versioning and deprecation as described in the previous section.
- **Choosing inappropriate HTTP status codes**: Developers use 200, 400, and 500 status codes all the time instead of using the appropriate HTTP status code.
- **Messy and misinformation** in swagger documentation.
- **Overcomplicating:** The biggest pitfall for developers is making the API cumbersome and confusing. Keeping it simple isn't easy, but we must do it.

Conclusion

In this chapter, we reviewed the concepts and constraints of RESTful APIs. We learned what makes general APIs go from being just APIs into being RESTful APIs - the REST constraints. We elaborated on those constraints and saw their implementation during the chapter. We learned how to start an API – from the first step of designing architecture well, building proper documentation in OpenAPI using Swagger, and building the right structure for Go and RESTful API. Then, we started crafting a gin-gonic server using Go and implemented several standard capabilities for RESTful APIs, like pagination, filtering, rate limit, and so on. Finally, we discussed conventions around RESTful APIs and how to version and deprecate the API when needed. While doing so, we remind ourselves of the common pitfalls that can happen when RESTful newcomers write APIs.

In the next chapter, we'll explore a crucial aspect of the service cycle in microservices architecture: the deployment phase. We'll explore the deployment phase while using the best technology in the market for that - Kubernetes.

References

- https://restfulapi.net/
- https://ics.uci.edu/~fielding/pubs/dissertation/rest_arch_style.htm
- https://trends.google.com/trends/explore?date=all&q=REST&hl=en-GB
- https://stripe.com/docs/api
- https://www.twilio.com/docs/api
- https://www.baeldung.com/cs/uniform-resource-identifiers
- https://swagger.io/
- https://github.com/go-gorm/gorm
- https://github.com/gin-gonic/gin
- https://pkg.go.dev/net/http
- https://go.dev/doc/tutorial/web-service-gin
- https://medium.easyread.co/how-to-do-pagination-in-postgres-with-golang-in-4-common-ways-12365b9fb528
- https://www.atatus.com/blog/rest-api-design-filtering-sorting-and-pagination/
- https://developer.mozilla.org/en-US/docs/Web/HTTP/Headers/Cache-Control
- https://medium.com/@nadinCodeHat/rest-api-naming-conventions-and-best-practices-1c4e781eb6a5
- https://readwrite.com/api-design-patterns-best-practices-for-building-resilient-apis/#:~:text=REST%20API%20Design%20Patterns&text=CRUD%20(Create%2C%20Read%2C%20Update,for%20resource%20discovery%20and%20navigation.
- https://codedamn.com/news/backend/rest-api-versioning-best-practices

CHAPTER 8
Introduction to Kubernetes

Introduction

Before talking about Kubernetes, there is a fundamental technology that needs to be explained first, which is Docker. Docker is a platform that uses OS-level virtualization to operate packed software called containers. These containers encapsulate an application and its dependencies, ensuring consistency across various environments. As developers, we must get familiar with the basic terms of containerization - image, container, and so on. And learn the basic syntax of the Docker file: https://docs.docker.com/engine/reference/builder/. If you aren't familiar with virtualization and containerization, it is recommended reading about them in more detail.

In a world where developers develop many services as part of bigger microservices architecture, they usually package those services into deliverable units called containers, which leads to a world where we need to manage enormous amounts of containers. It is almost impossible to manage and operate this number of containers while supporting each developer's needs and specific requirements. Fortunately, some folks at Google saw this coming problem and crafted a single project to resolve it. This project is called Kubernetes.

Why should we learn Kubernetes? "*I need to write my code and let the operation side (usually DevOps) do all the other work for me.*" This answer would be acceptable in a perfect world, but it isn't the case. There is a coupling between the application and the way it is deployed. As developers, we must ensure our functionality happens as expected in production. There is a vast difference between the local and production environments – different parameters, edge cases we didn't think of, scale issues, security concerns, and more. To mitigate problems in that difference, we as developers need to know the basics about Kubernetes - common resources, rollout procedure, troubleshooting, central best practices, monitoring, and so on. In this chapter, we are going to explore those topics.

What is the relation between Kubernetes and microservices architecture?

In simple words, Kubernetes is solving many issues and downsides of microservices architecture. For example, using an external configuration in a microservices architecture is recommended. Kubernetes solves it by providing ConfigMaps and Secrets (storage resources) to inject data into the application containers. That is why the combination of the two is powerful.

Another example is that routing capabilities can be implemented efficiently using Ingress (Kubernetes resource).

Kubernetes is an open-source container orchestration system. This system was invented by Google in 2014 and is now maintained by the CNCF (Cloud Native Computing Foundation). A shortcut for Kubernetes is K8s (due to the 8 letters between K and S).

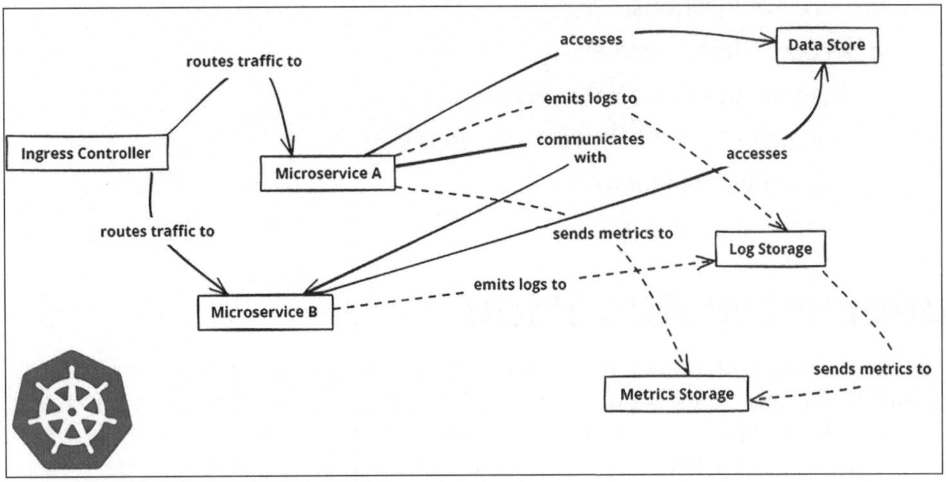

Figure 8.1: *Microservices architecture uses Kubernetes example*

Structure

In this chapter, we will discuss the following topics:

- Kubernetes Adoption
- Kubernetes Essential Tools - **`kind, kubectl, kubectx`**
- Basic Resources
  - Node
  - Namespace
  - Pod
- Workloads Management
  - Deployment
  - DaemonSet
  - StatefulSet
  - Job

  - CronJob
- Important Resources
  - ConfigMap
  - Secret
  - HPA
  - Ingress
- Readiness and Liveness Probes
- Resources Allocations
- Kubernetes Best Practices
  - Maintaining Good YAML Hygiene
  - Logging - Specifically for Kubernetes
  - Environments Management
  - Proper Monitoring

Kubernetes Adoption

Nowadays, Kubernetes is widely used, and most companies in the world use it. The community of Kubernetes is enormous and keeps growing year after year. There are a considerable number of conferences worldwide whose topic is only Kubernetes. There are tons of open-source projects and tools that are related to Kubernetes.

Furthermore, some companies have products that are natively for Kubernetes. It is already industry standard to use Kubernetes as the place to deploy our services and workloads.

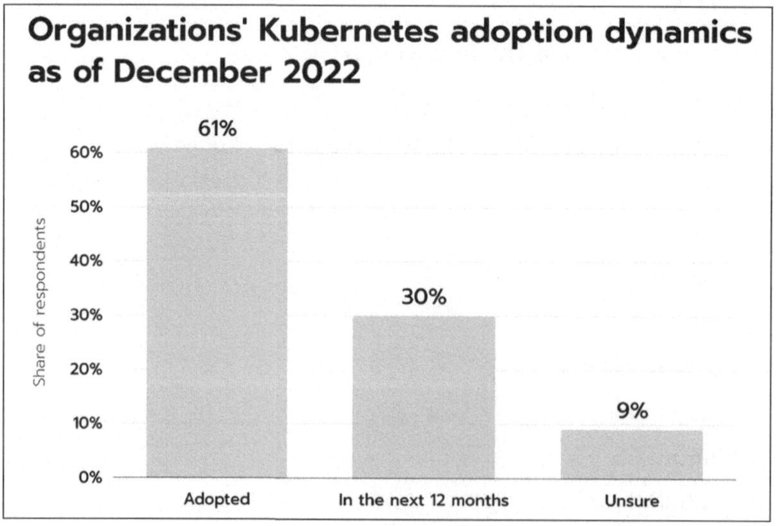

Figure 8.2: *Kubernetes Adoption December 2022*

Kubernetes aims to manage containerized workloads and services. Moreover, the goal is to automate the complex procedure of deployment. Kubernetes takes care of several aspects regarding the deployment process - networking, configuration, rollout, and so on – and also takes care of the management - storage, security, and so on.

Kubernetes composes several tools and projects inside it and leverages the power of each one of them. For example, Kubernetes uses Docker as the container runtime engine and doesn't have its own container runtime engine. Kubernetes comes as a single unit called - **cluster**. We can create resources in that cluster by defining the desired resources. We'll configure the desired resource that we want using YAML. Kubernetes will perform all the other work for us and strive to reach the desired state we defined. Further in this chapter, we'll elaborate on the different Kubernetes resources relevant to software engineers.

Kubernetes Essential Tools

Let's discuss some necessary tools of Kubernetes:

Kind

Kind stands for Kubernetes IN Docker, a tool for running a Kubernetes cluster as a Docker container. It is straightforward and usually used for local or testing environments because it is lightweight and easy to use. Other tools that do the same are Minikube and K3s. Here is how we can start a cluster using **`kind`**:

```
kind create cluster --name example
```

Kubectl

Kubectl is a tool that is part of the Kubernetes OSS project. It is a CLI that lets us interact easily with Kubernetes API. Here are some common commands of **`kubectl`**:

Get resources:

```
kubectl get pods
```

```
kubectl get nodes --output json
```

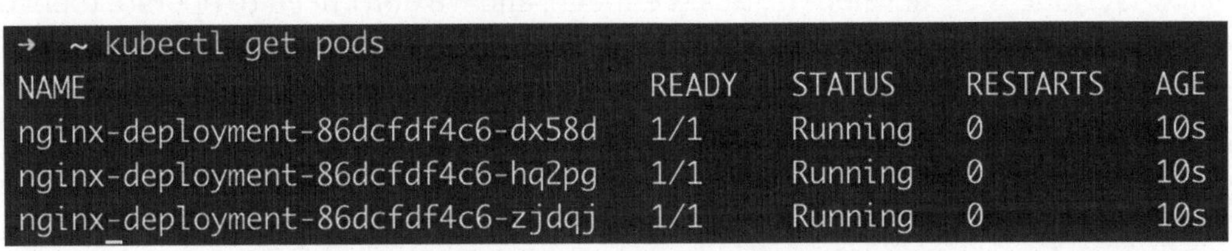

Figure 8.3: *kubectl get pods output sample response*

The first example shows how to get all pods in the cluster in the default namespace. The second example gets all the nodes in the cluster with the output format of JSON.

Create a new resource:

```
kubectl create -f pod.yaml
```

Modify/Create a resource:

```
kubectl apply -f pod.yaml
```

Delete a pod called frontend:

```
kubectl delete pods/frontend
```

To see all the commands **kubectl** has, we can run:

```
kubectl help
kubectl help <command-name>
```

Kubectx

Minimalist CLI tool that helps us to switch between clusters. When we use **kubectl**, it goes to the cluster API declared in the **~/.kube** directory. By using **kubectx**, it just switches the context to the desired cluster. For example:

```
kubectx <cluster-name>
```

Basic Resources

The following three resources are widely used in Kubernetes. It is essential to know what they are to understand Kubernetes. We'll mention them repeatedly in this chapter.

Node

"A Node *is a worker machine in Kubernetes and may be either a virtual or a physical machine, depending on the cluster. Each Node is managed by the control plane. A Node can have multiple pods, and the Kubernetes control plane automatically handles scheduling the pods across the Nodes in the cluster.*"

This is a quote from official Kubernetes documentation. This quote explains pretty well what Node is. As developers, this is enough, and we don't need to operate them or tackle node issues. However, note that sometimes our application will have a problem due to node issues. At the very least, we need to understand that the issue is related to the node and transfer it to the operation person to tackle it.

Namespace

Namespaces in Kubernetes are a mechanism of separation and isolation between resources. Some resources can be namespaced, and some are not. Each time we get resources using **kubectl get**, it will bring us all the resources from the **default** namespace unless we specify differently; by adding **-A**, we can get all resources in all namespaces. Names of resources and kinds need to be unique inside a namespace. To see which resources are namespaced and which aren't, we can run:

```
kubectl api-resources
```

```
→ ~ kubectl api-resources
NAME                 SHORTNAMES   APIVERSION   NAMESPACED   KIND
bindings                          v1           true         Binding
componentstatuses    cs           v1           false        ComponentStatus
configmaps           cm           v1           true         ConfigMap
```

Figure 8.4: *kubectl api-resources output*

Note the column "**NAMESPACED**", which gives a boolean answer if the resource kind is namespaced.

Pod

Pod resources are the smallest deployable unit in Kubernetes. A Pod is a set of containers with shared volumes, environment, and context. We'll probably not need to deploy a Pod alone; a Pod is usually part of the running workload. However, most investigations will be around the pod, describing it, getting its logs, or getting basic data about the Pod.

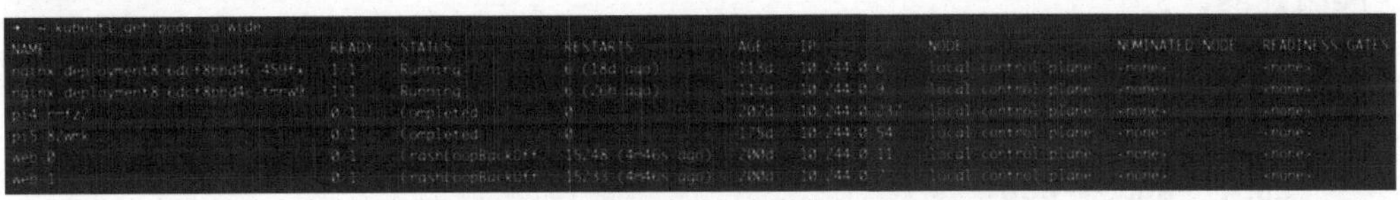

Figure 8.5: *get pods while using wide output*

Describe a pod:

```
kubectl describe pods/nginx-deployment8-6dcf8bbd4c-459fx
```

Describe a pod is a typical command; it gives us many details regarding the Pod and the last events of the Pod. We can also use the **describe** command for any other resource in the following format –

```
kubectl describe <resource-kind>/<resource-name>
```

See the logs:

```
kubectl logs pods/frontend2
```

Like the **describe** command, we can use the **logs** command for each resource, but it is less valuable.

Workload Management

A workload is an application running on Kubernetes. The workload is a service in a microservices architecture. As we have already seen, deploying and managing service (workload) is challenging, complicated, and requires much work. Kubernetes provides solutions for deploying and managing service through workload resources. Here, we'll present and explain about the built-in workload resources.

Deployment

Deployment is the most common workload in Kubernetes. Deployment is used to manage stateless services. Pods that are being managed by Deployment are volatile. When a pod is terminated (whether an issue or rollout causes it), the Deployment resource creates another new pod with a different name. Deployment uses a resource called ReplicaSet to manage the pods. Each time we release a new version (just applying new YAML), a new ReplicaSet is being created and is replacing the old ReplicaSet and old pods.

```yaml
apiVersion: apps/v1
kind: Deployment
metadata:
  name: random-deployment
spec:
  replicas: 3
  selector:
    matchLabels:
      app: random-app
  template:
    metadata:
      labels:
        app: random-app
    spec:
      containers:
      - name: random-container
        image: nginx:latest
        ports:
        - containerPort: 80
```

The preceding YAML is an example of minimal Deployment YAML in Kubernetes.

DaemonSet

DaemonSet is a workload that is suitable for running pods on nodes. The goal of DaemonSet is to provide facilities that are relevant to local nodes. For example,

DaemonSet with one replica will schedule one pod on each node in the cluster. Use cases can be storage daemons, network-related daemons, logs aggregators, telemetry daemons, and others.

StatefulSet

StatefulSet is a workload resource designed for pods that require persistent state or unique identities. Unlike Deployment resources, where pods are interchangeable and ephemeral, StatefulSets ensure that pods are recreated with the same name and state after termination. StatefulSet provides a consistent volume that the pods can attach to using other resources called PV (PersistentVolume) and PVC (PersistentVolumeClaim). Use cases for StatefulSet can be database services, messaging systems, and so on.

Job

Job resource allows us to define a task that can run until it is completed. It's as simple as that. Jobs resources can be used, for example, for data processing.

CronJob

It is a way to run Job resource but with a cron scheduler wrapping it. Usage cases of CronJob resources can be maintenance tasks, scheduled backups, batch processing, and so on.

```
apiVersion: batch/v1beta1
kind: CronJob
metadata:
  name: random-cronjob
spec:
  schedule: "*/5 * * * *"  # Runs every 5 minutes
  jobTemplate:
    spec:
      template:
        metadata:
          labels:
            app: random-cronjob
        spec:
          containers:
          - name: random-container
            image: busybox
```

```
          command: ["echo", "Hello from the cronjob!"]
        restartPolicy: OnFailure
```

In the preceding YAML example, we can see CronJob YAML; note that inside the CronJob YAML, we define a Job YAML and wrap it with a scheduler.

Important Resources

The following resources are common when using Kubernetes; we may encounter them as developers.

ConfigMap

ConfigMap is a resource that stores non-confidential data in key-value pairs. Pods can consume ConfigMap data through environment variables, arguments, or volumes. ConfigMap helps us achieve one of the elements of microservices: external configuration. Data that can be stored in ConfigMap includes app properties, connection strings, environment data, endpoints, and so on.

```
apiVersion: v1
kind: ConfigMap
metadata:
  name: random-configmap
data:
  app_name: my-app
  database_url: "mongodb://localhost:27017"
```

The preceding YAML example describes ConfigMap.

Secret

Secret resources are just like ConfigMap resources, but store sensitive data instead of non-sensitive data. Data that can be stored in Secrets includes passwords, API keys, certificates, and so on.

HPA

HPA, which stands for Horizontal Pod Autoscaling, is a resource used to auto-scale workload resources (not suited for all workloads). Horizontal auto scaling means scaling is done by increasing or decreasing the number of replicas (Pods). The scaling is based on metrics (CPU or memory) and their desired values. In HPA configuration, there are minimum and maximum pod amounts. We will often use HPA for services on a dynamic scale and a load that occasionally differs.

Ingress

"Ingress exposes HTTP and HTTPS routes from outside the cluster to services within the cluster. Traffic routing is controlled by rules defined on the Ingress resource."

In the quote, the term "**services**" refers specifically to a Kubernetes resource named "**service**." This resource is responsible for networking within the Kubernetes environment and should not be confused with the broader concept of services, especially in the context of microservices.

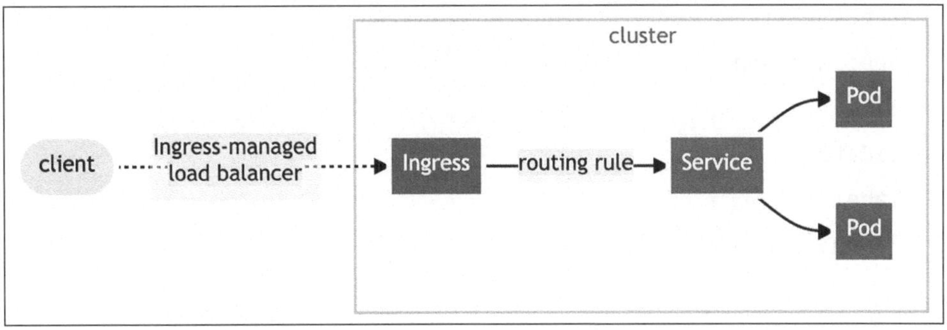

Figure 8.6: *Ingress resource in Kubernetes*

This is the most complicated resource we'll mention in this chapter. As developers, we'll probably encounter Ingress only when we want to add a new route or change a route. Lastly, please note that the Ingress resource solves some of the significant concerns of API Gateway (core element in microservices architecture), such as load balancing, security, and high-level routing.

Readiness and Liveness Probes

In Kubernetes, a Pod receives traffic when all containers are running. Also, when Kubernetes detects that a Pod is crashing (due to exit code or other failures), it restarts it. These detections, whether a Pod is ready to receive traffic or needs to be restarted, are automatically resolved by Kubernetes. However, in some scenarios, we, as developers, will want to provide additional information for Kubernetes to perform those detections. For example, we can decide that a Pod can't receive traffic until it establishes a connection to the DB. Another example can be when we wish to restart a pod if we figure that the Pod cache is invalid. The way to perform that manual detection is readiness and liveness probes.

- **Readiness probe**: Indicated whether the container is ready to accept traffic and requests.
- **Liveness probe**: Indicates whether the container is operated. If not, it needs to be killed and restarted.

```yaml
apiVersion: apps/v1
kind: Deployment
metadata:
  name: web-app-deployment
spec:
  replicas: 3
  selector:
    matchLabels:
      app: web-app
  template:
    metadata:
      labels:
        app: web-app
    spec:
      containers:
      - name: web-app-container
        image: nginx:latest
        ports:
        - containerPort: 80
        readinessProbe:
          httpGet:
            path: /healthz
            port: 80
          initialDelaySeconds: 5
          periodSeconds: 10
        livenessProbe:
          httpGet:
            path: /status
            port: 80
          initialDelaySeconds: 10
          periodSeconds: 15
```

The preceding YAML example illustrates Deployment YAML using a readiness probe to check if the container is healthy and a liveness probe to check the status of the container if it is working as expected.

There are various ways to define probes. It can be a request to a specific endpoint using HTTP, TCP socket, shell command, and so on. An HTTP GET request is the most common use case (like the example).

Developers need to configure and write the probes themselves because we are the only ones who can determine when the application can accept traffic and when it needs to be restarted.

Resources Allocations

When specifying Pods in Kubernetes or Pods within workloads, we can optionally specify how many resources we can allocate to the container. The standard and frequent resources allocated are CPU and memory, but there are more. We can specify two parameters for resource allocation - **`request`** and **`limit`**.

- **`Request`**: When defining resource **`requests`**, the scheduler uses that to decide which node to place a Pod. The **`request`** is resource usage expectations.
- **`Limit`**: When defining resource limit, the **`kubelet`** ("node agent") enforces the **`limit`** and doesn't let the container pass those **`limits`**. If the CPU reaches the **`limit`**, the container will be throttled; if the memory reaches the **`limit`**, the Pod the container runs on will be killed and restarted.

It is crucial to be on top of the resources we allocate. Without proper allocation, Pods can do whatever they want. For example, our application can have memory leaks and consume tons of memory, affecting the other Pods on the Node or the entire cluster. Another example from the other side is that small memory allocation can limit our application from operating correctly. As developers, we are responsible for determining the amount of resources our containers need.

Here is an example of Pod YAML starting a container named **`hello`** with **`requests`** and **`limits`** of CPU and memory:

```
apiVersion: v1
kind: Pod
metadata:
  name: example
spec:
  containers:
  - name: hello
    image: hello-world:latest
    resources:
      requests:
        memory: "128Mi"
```

```
    cpu: "250m"
  limits:
    memory: "256Mi"
    cpu: "1"
```

Kubernetes Best Practices

The following four best practices are more relevant to Kubernetes developers. Several other best practices are more relevant to operations. A book recommended for more detailed best practices in Kubernetes is *Kubernetes Patterns*. There is a link to it in the references. These patterns aren't taken from this book.

Maintaining Good YAML Hygiene

YAMLs are everything when it comes to Kubernetes. YAMLs are the desired state in Kubernetes. As users, we define them, and Kubernetes does all the other work for us. It strives to transform the current state to the desired state (the YAML file). With that understanding, the YAML must answer the following requirements:

- **Neat and Clean:** It doesn't contain any configuration we don't need or want. Also, we need to avoid declaring default configurations in YAML files.
- **Labels and Annotations:** Those two terms are metadata related to the YAML resource. Annotations are used for arbitrary metadata, and labels are used to identify resources in Kubernetes. This is a vast topic in Kubernetes, but we won't discuss it here. We need to leverage the usage of those two metadata in each YAML file.
- **For Workloads**: Specify **liveness and readiness probes**, as we mentioned earlier.
- **ConfigMaps and Secrets Must be Adequately Configured:** Never redeclare a key value already declared in an existing ConfigMap or Secret.

Logging – Specifically for Kubernetes

There are slight differences in how we use logs in Kubernetes compared to how we use them in other systems. To avoid mistakes, we must tag and label logs properly by including:

- **Proper service name**: Not the Pod name! We must include the service name in the log so we'll be able to correlate logs to the same service. A common mistake is that logs only include the instance name (Pod name in the case of Kubernetes) instead of the service name.
- **Version**: To determine when things changed in which version, we must specify the service version on each log. By doing so, we can see and observe the

lifecycle of our service. For example, a log of errors started occurring only in version 1.3.2, which means that a bug was started in this version.

- **Cluster environment information**: Any data that might affect the behavior of our application. Sometimes, our service isn't guilty of having an issue or error. The cluster or Node might be responsible for that issue. For example, logging the Node name can be very useful.

Environments Management

In any system, we'll have different environments for different reasons. Production environment, staging environment (sometimes called pre-production), testing environment, local environment, and so on. There are two approaches to separating environments in Kubernetes:

- **Different clusters for each environment**: The main advantage of this approach is that the environments are decoupled and don't have dependencies between them. Its main disadvantage is that it takes much more effort to set up a different cluster for each environment and much more effort to maintain several clusters.
- **Different namespaces for each environment**: This approach has the opposite advantages and disadvantages of the previous approach. While there are dependencies between the environments (Pods from different environments can be allocated on the same Node, for example), it takes much less effort to set up and maintain.

Proper Monitoring

In addition to the regular monitoring we as developers tend to put on services, there is monitoring relevant for services running on Kubernetes. Here are three significant things to monitor:

- **Resources**: Monitor the usage of CPU, memory, and storage. It is essential to monitor these resources to optimize service performance, identify bottlenecks, and ensure efficient resource allocation.
- **Containers Status**: Monitor whether the containers are down/up/errors/probes/restart count, and so on. These metrics are essential to ensure reliability and the health of the services. Furthermore, they help detect issues, facilitate troubleshooting, and contribute to more stable and resilient services.
- **Kubernetes Events**: Kubernetes audits the actions he takes through events. Kubernetes events are drawing the history of the cluster. By monitoring Kubernetes events, we can detect trends, problems, and anomalies and gain many insights by looking at the events.

Conclusion

In this chapter, we went through the basics of Kubernetes and focused on the resources and actions more relevant to developers, not the operation side. We covered the three basic terms in Kubernetes - Node, Pod, and Namespace. These terms give the base for understanding other resources in Kubernetes. We learned about Kubernetes workloads - Deployment, DaemonSet, StatefulSet, Jon, and CronJob. As developers, we must choose the right workload resource for a service. After that, we covered common Kubernetes resources we'll probably encounter while working with Kubernetes - ConfigMap, Secret, HPA, and Ingress.

Then, we discussed two major Kubernetes concepts pertinent to developers. The first was readiness and liveness probes, which ensure our service is ready to work (accepting traffic) and running properly. The second is resource allocation – we learned what needs to be specified when working with workloads (mainly requests and limits for CPU and memory).

Finally, we went through four best practices that are super relevant for developers using Kubernetes - maintaining YAML hygiene, environment management, logging, and monitoring specific to Kubernetes.

In the next chapter, we'll take the accumulated knowledge from this chapter and the previous chapters into production. We'll leverage Kubernetes capabilities to learn how to deploy services to the production environment while maintaining the microservices architecture style.

References

- https://www.avenga.com/magazine/running-kubernetes-on-premise-versus-in-the-cloud/
- https://goteleport.com/blog/microservices-containers-kubernetes/
- https://kind.sigs.k8s.io/
- https://minikube.sigs.k8s.io/docs/start/
- https://k3s.io/
- https://kubernetes.io/docs/reference/kubectl/
- https://kubernetes.io/docs/tutorials/kubernetes-basics/explore/explore-intro/#:~:text=A%20Node%20is%20a%20worker,the%20Nodes%20in%20the%20cluster.
- https://kubernetes.io/docs/concepts/services-networking/ingress/
- https://www.oreilly.com/library/view/kubernetes-patterns/9781492050278/

CHAPTER 9
Deploying to Production

Introduction

This chapter will focus on the critical things we must do when deploying our applications or services to production. After finishing writing the code and all the business logic, our service is "**seemingly**" ready to be deployed. Why seemingly?

Addressing potential issues in advance is crucial to ensuring a smooth and secure transition to production. This involves several **preparations**, including rollout procedure, thorough testing, and precise packaging, to ensure our services meet expectations when deployed. Most importantly, the application must pass security measures to protect against vulnerabilities and threats before deployment to production. This includes implementing encryption, access controls, and regular security audits to safeguard sensitive data and maintain the integrity of the application.

In this chapter, we'll delve into the essential preparations required for a successful transition to production, introducing several widely recognized and proven techniques in the software industry. We'll see how these techniques can be implemented using Golang, from security basics and CI/CD to failures design best practices and deployment strategies.

Structure

In this chapter, we will discuss the following topics:

- CI/CD
- Design of Failures
  - Timeouts
  - Retries
  - Fallback
  - Circuit Breaker
  - Bulkhead

- Security
    - Authentication
    - Authorization
- Feature Toggling
- Rollouts
    - Basic Deployment
    - Rolling Update
    - Blue-Green Deployment
    - Multi-Service Rollout
    - Canary Deployment
- Rollbacks

CI/CD

CI/CD, which stands for continuous integration and continuous delivery (or continuous deployment), is not just a set of tools; it's a cultural shift that empowers teams to deliver better software faster and more reliably.

Before the DevOps era, the application and software release cycle was monthly, quarterly, annually, and even longer. In the DevOps era, due to CI/CD culture, integrating a new code life cycle is much faster – it can be a few releases in a single day or a few releases every hour. As developers, as fast as we deliver our code and integrate it with the real world (production environment), we can gain a faster feedback loop and, therefore, detect bugs, fixes, and improvements faster.

- **Continuous Integration (CI):** Focuses on frequent code integration and automated testing.
- **Continuous Delivery (CD):** Adds automated packaging deployment to environments such as production and staging.
- **Continuous Deployment (CD):** Releases changes directly to production without manual intervention

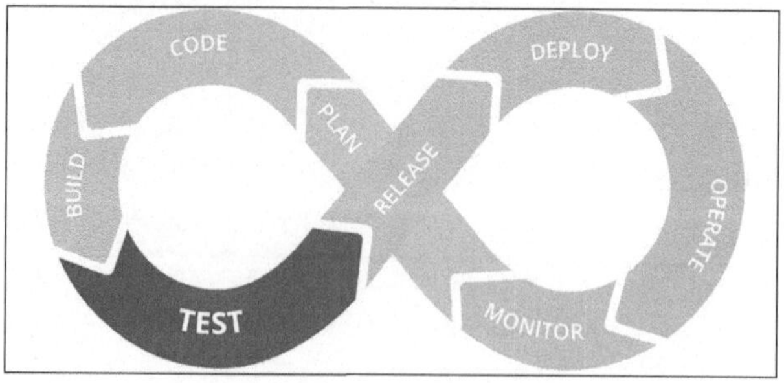

Figure 9.1: *CI/CD lifecycle*

The preceding figure describes the CI/CD pipeline's lifecycle with the general steps included inside.

In particular, CI refers to the process before the point of deploying the code to production. The figure represents the blue colors (plan, code, build, and test). The CI's main job is to package and test the code. If the CI is adequately passed, it will continue to the CD. CD refers to deploying the code into other environments (mainly production). The CD process strives to be fully automated and without any manual interaction.

Various market tools help create CI/CD pipelines, such as Jenkins, GitHub actions, CircleCI, and more. As developers, we won't create these pipelines but must be aware of them and ensure our code is being tested, built, and deployed as we want.

Using CI/CD pipelines is crucial in a microservices architecture for two main reasons:

- **Maintaining Consistency:** A consistent and automated deployment process ensures that all the services can continue working together seamlessly.
- **Scalability:** As the system grows, the number of services will increase. Usually, increasing the number of services will increase the amount of work linearly. However, due to CI/CD, the amount of work will be much less when more services are added.

Design of Failures

When deploying an application into production, there is fog and uncertainty regarding how it will act. Although our code passed unit tests or even a smoke test, it is possible and common for our application to encounter bugs and errors. We need to be prepared for those scenarios. We'll discover several valuable ways and design patterns to handle failures while having RESTful API services in a microservices architecture.

Timeouts

Timeouts are essential for any service that needs to send a request to another service or if it needs bound execution time for some piece of software. We'll often use timeouts when sending a request from one service to another. Using timeouts, we avoid unnecessary on-flight requests that can overload the services. The timeout time differs between each service, usually between 10 and 60 seconds with an average of 30 seconds, but it depends on the scenario and basically can be any selected time limit. Let's see an example of implementing timeouts in Golang.

** *Disclaimer–The timeout is arbitrary, and the number I gave is from my POV as an engineer. It can defer, be a maximum of 5 seconds, or last a few minutes.*

The following examples illustrate how to implement timeouts in Go using channels. In the first example, a timeout occurs, while in the second example, it does not. We begin by creating a channel with a capacity of 1, followed by a goroutine that simulates a delay and then sends a message to the channel. After the goroutine is launched, we use a select statement to either print the result from the channel if it arrives before the timeout or print "**Timeout**" if the timeout is reached first:

```
// Example with timeout
resultCh := make(chan string, 1)
go func() {
	time.Sleep(3 * time.Second)
	resultCh <- "Received before timeout"
}()

select {
case res := <-resultCh:
	println(res)
case <-time.After(2 * time.Second):
	println("Timeout")
}

// Output: Timeout

// Example without timeout
resultCh = make(chan string, 1)
go func() {
	time.Sleep(1 * time.Second)
	resultCh <- "Received before timeout"
}()

select {
case res := <-resultCh:
	println(res)
case <-time.After(2 * time.Second):
	println("Timeout")
}

// Output: Received before timeout
```

In these examples, the **select** statement is used to handle the timing, checking if the result from the channel is received before the specified timeout period.

We can also implement timeouts using context. Let's see how:

```
ctx, _ := context.WithTimeout(context.Background(), 2*time.Second)
go func() {
select {
	case <-ctx.Done():
		println("Timeout")
		os.Exit(1)
	}
}()

time.Sleep(3 * time.Second)
fmt.Println("Done")
```

Similar to the earlier example, we also implemented a timeout mechanism in this example, but we used **context.WithTimeout** and **Done()** functions. In this example, the **Done()** function sends a signal into the channel when the timeout occurs.

Retries

As discussed in the previous chapters, in microservices architecture, the common communication between services is through API calls. Eventually, API calls will fail, and we must handle these failures. A simple retry can often solve the issue and decrease the error rate significantly (unless this is a bug that will occur anyway). A good practice is to perform approximately two retries (in addition to the first try). The number of retries still depends on the use case, which can be 0 or more.

Another good practice is to wait between each retry using an exponential backoff algorithm. The exponential backoff algorithm is a strategy used to gradually increase the delay between retry attempts in case of failures, reducing the load on the system and improving the chances of successful communication.

For example, the waiting time between each retry is 1,2,4,8,16, and so on. Let's see an example of exponential back-off retries in action in Golang.

```
func main() {
	err := Retry(3, time.Second, func() error {
		fmt.Println("trying...")
		return fmt.Errorf("some error")
	})
```

```
	if err != nil {
		fmt.Printf("error: %s\n", err)
	}
}

func Retry(attempts int, sleep time.Duration, f func() error) (err error) {
	currentAttempt := 1
	for {
		err = f()
		if err == nil {
			return nil
		}
		if currentAttempt >= attempts {
			return fmt.Errorf("after %d attempts, last error: 
%w", attempts, err)
		}
		time.Sleep(sleep)
		sleep *= 2
		currentAttempt++
	}
}
```

```
The output:
trying...
trying...
trying...
error: after 3 attempts, last error: some error
```

In the preceding example, there is a specific implementation of exponential back-off retries. We can implement retries in many other forms. For example, we can also write a specific retries mechanism for requests between services.

Fallback

In a scenario where we can experience a failure, we must handle that failure. We can try to perform retries like in the previous section. However, it can't always solve the problem, and we need a fallback that we can trust. Fallback is a known function executed without any error or a previous functionality we can trust. In the worst case, a **fallback** will inform the user that something went wrong.

```
func main() {
	result, err := performOperation()
	if err != nil {
		// Fallback operation in case of an error
		result = fallbackOperation()
	}

	fmt.Println("Result:", result)
}

func performOperation() (string, error) {
	return "", fmt.Errorf("Operation failed")
}

func fallbackOperation() string {
	return "Fallback result"
}
```

In the preceding example, we showed a simple way to perform fallback. We try to use the **performOperation()** function. Still, unfortunately, it has an error, so we use a fallback function called **fallbackOperation()**, which has a constant result.

Circuit Breaker

A circuit breaker is a design pattern used to enhance the resilience and stability of distributed systems, in our case – microservices architecture. It helps prevent cascading failures (failure of one service causes many services to fail, like dominoes) by detecting and handling faults in a controlled manner.

The circuit breaker monitors the availability of a service and, if it detects a certain threshold of failures, "*opens*" the circuit, preventing further calls to the failing service. This allows the system to gracefully handle failures, reduce load on the troubled service, and prevent degradation of the entire system. There are several ways to implement a circuit breaker, but using an existing library like https://github.com/sony/gobreaker is recommended.

Let's dive deep into the logic and behavior of this pattern. There are three states that the circuit breaker can have: Closed, Open, and Half-Open.

Closed

This is also the initial state of the circuit breaker.

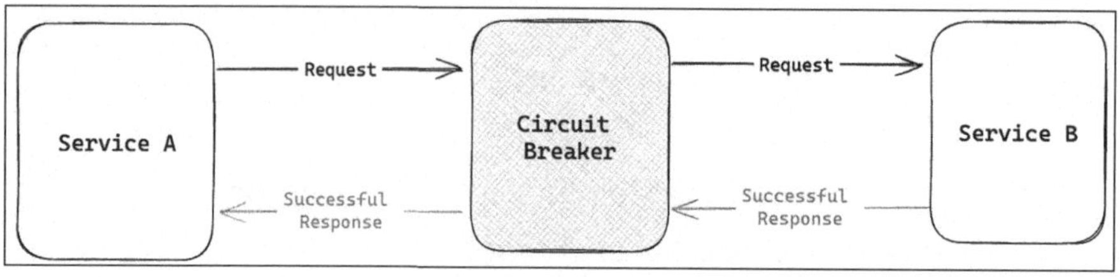

Figure 9.2: *Circuit Breaker in Closed State*

In this state, the circuit breaker allows requests from service A to service B. While doing so, the circuit breaker monitors the number of failures by defined periods (10 failures per minute, for example). If the number of failures in a period exceeds the defined threshold, the state becomes Open.

Open

Figure 9.3 shows the open state:

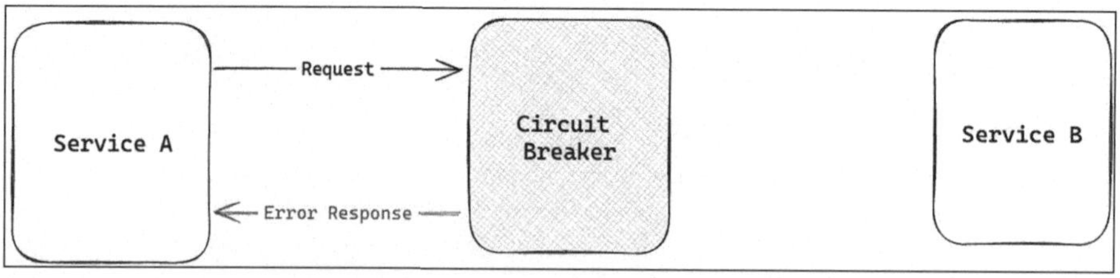

Figure 9.3: *Circuit Breaker in Open State*

In this state, the circuit breaker will block any request from service A and return an error response to service A. Meanwhile, service B won't receive any requests. The circuit breaker will remain open until a defined timeout period ends. Then, it will go into Half-Open state.

Half-Open

Figure 9.4 depicts the half-open state:

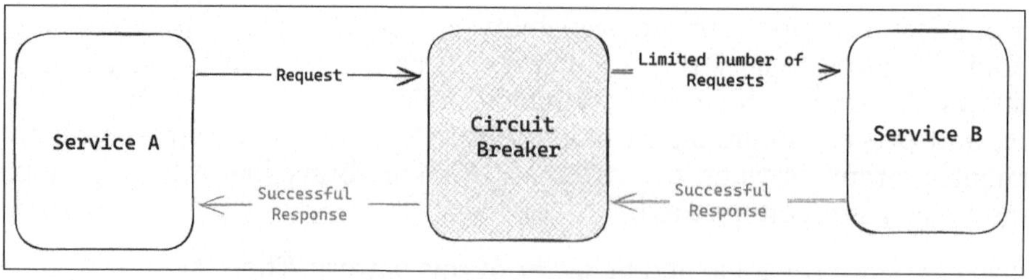

Figure 9.4: *Circuit Breaker in Half-Open State*

In this state, the circuit breaker will allow limited requests to go from service A to service B. If those limited number of requests are successful, the circuit breaker will switch again to a Closed state.

Bulkhead

Like the circuit breaker pattern, the bulkhead pattern aims to keep the system resilient and avoid cascading failures. This pattern is inspired by ship bulkheads that compartmentalize sections to avoid water leaks.

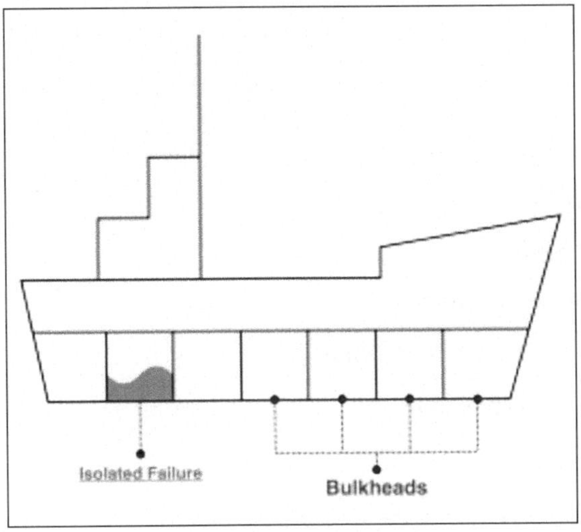

***Figure* 9.5:** *Ship bulkheads*

In software, bulkhead pattern isolates components or services, limiting the impact of failures in one service from affecting others. This pattern is instrumental in concurrent (at the service level) or distributed systems (at the system level), where it helps maintain system stability by isolating and controlling the failures within distinct services, minimizing the risk of cascading failures.

We implement a bulkhead pattern at the system level by deploying multiple replicas per workload. It is essential to have as many truly isolated service instances as possible. Take cache as an example; we would prefer to have a separate cache per replica instead of a single cache for all replicas. Now, a problem caused by one replica will affect all the other replicas (through the cache).

At the service level, we'll want goroutines to operate with as minimal dependencies as possible between them. Moreover, we'll often want to limit the number of concurrent goroutines to avoid a lot of load on the service, leading to its collapse. We have already seen the usage of waiting for concurrent goroutines to finish using **`sync.WaitGroup`**. However, we didn't enforce a hard limit regarding the maximum number of concurrent goroutines. A good implementation for limiting the number of goroutines can be using a package called **`sizedwaitgroup`** - https://github.com/remeh/sizedwaitgroup. Let's see how to use it.

```
package main

import (
	"fmt"
	"time"

	"github.com/remeh/sizedwaitgroup"
)

func main() {
	swg := sizedwaitgroup.New(5)
	for i := 0; i < 100; i++ {
		swg.Add()
		go func(i int) {
			defer swg.Done()
			logic(i)
		}(i)
	}

	swg.Wait()
}

func logic(i int) {
	fmt.Println(i)
	time.Sleep(1 * time.Second)
}
```

In the preceding code example, we set a "special **WaitGroup**" from a package called **sizedwaitgroup** using a function called **New** that accepts the maximum number of goroutines as a numeric parameter. After that, we use a for-loop that iterates over the numbers 0-99. Then, like a normal **WaitGroup**, we use the **Add()** function to declare that goroutine is starting.

Inside the goroutine, we execute the **logic** function that prints the number and sleeps for a second, then says the goroutine finished its work using the **Done()** function. The final result is an output that will print all the numbers in batches of 5 elements each time and wait a second between each batch.

Security

In this chapter, we'll discuss security around services in a nutshell – mainly from the developer's point of view - authentication and authorization. It is essential to deploy secured services to production to prevent access from malicious threats – but we won't be looking into the security manners that need to be taken as part of the operation. This is mainly because it is the responsibility of the operation, not the developers.

In any microservices system, we'll want to guarantee access only to the system users.

Moreover, each user usually has specific and different access restrictions. To achieve those two, we must implement authentication and authorization.

Authentication

"Authentication verifies that you are who you say you are or that something you own is not a forgery. It might involve verifying documents, asking for input from you, or both."

This is a quote from Okta that describes authentication well.

Several options are available for implementing authentication in a web application, ranging from using third-party services to implementing authentication services yourself. Here are some examples:

- **Third-Party Services**
  - **Auth0**: Auth0 provides authentication and authorization as a service.
  - **Firebase Authentication**: Firebase provides a suite of services for building web and mobile applications, including authentication.
- **Self-Implemented Authentication**
  - **JWT (aka for JSON Web Token)**: We can implement authentication using JWTs. JWTs are encoded tokens that contain a set of claims that can be used to authenticate users.
  - **Session-Based Authentication**: We can implement authentication using sessions and cookies. When a user logs in, a session is created on the server, and a session ID is stored in a cookie on the client. Subsequent requests include the session ID, which the server uses to authenticate the user.
- **Libraries/Frameworks**
  - **Passport.js**: Passport.js is a popular authentication middleware for Node.js.
  - **Spring Security**: Spring Security is a powerful and highly customizable authentication and access control framework for Java applications.

Authorization

"Authorization in system security is the process of giving the user permission to access a specific resource or function. This term is often used interchangeably with access control or client privilege." – Another quote from Okta describes authorization.

Unlike authentication, the authorization process demands us to implement business logic. Only when we know our system's resources and functions will the product team define what the users' permissions will look like. Each service in the system must enforce user permission using an authorization system when having a microservices architecture.

The problem is that we don't want to implement a separate authorization system for each service. Usually, the authorization logic is similar across the system, and we'll want to leverage it to create a central authorization service or shared code that contains the authorization logic. Whether we use an external authorization service or just a shared code, we'll inject the user permissions into the context of a single service using middleware.

Like many other capabilities we mentioned in *Chapter 7, Building RESTful* API, the middleware can use shared code or centralized authorization service depending on the need. We need to enforce the user permissions manually by code or do it more automatically at the DB level. Here are the use cases of using authorization:

- Giving access to endpoint **`POST /users`** only to account administrators.
- Giving access to endpoint **`GET /views`** to all users, **`UPDATE /views`** only to managers and administrators, **`DELETE /views`** only to administrators.

Feature Toggling

Another way to get confidence while deploying services to production is to use feature toggling. Feature toggling allows us to use flags (so-called feature flags) inside our service. Flags are dynamic values, usually a boolean, injected from other services in the service's runtime. Flags can have the ability to have different configurations for different users. Flags can be used for several purposes: testing new features, A/B testing, load testing, opening features only to specific users due to customer requirements, and so on.

Here are a few examples of flags:

- A Boolean flag named "*show-billing-tab-ui*" determines whether a UI tab named "**`billing`**" is opened. We can show the feature ("**`billing`**" tab) only to the product manager inside the company so they will approve or refine it before releasing it to all customers.
- A numeric flag named "**`pagination-size`**" determines the pagination size of an API, which can be used to test the optimal pagination size for the best performance.

```
func main() {
	if getEnvBool("feature-a", false) {
		fmt.Println("Feature A is enabled. Performing Feature A
		logic.")
		// Include Feature A logic here
	} else {
		fmt.Println("Feature A is not enabled.")
	}

	if getEnvBool("feature-b", false) {
		fmt.Println("Feature B is enabled. Performing Feature B
		logic.")
		// Include Feature B logic here
	} else {
		fmt.Println("Feature B is not enabled.")
	}

	// Rest of the application logic
}

func getEnvBool(flagName string, defaultValue bool) bool {
	value, exists := os.LookupEnv(flagName)
	if !exists {
		return defaultValue
	}

	result, err := strconv.ParseBool(value)
	if err != nil {
		fmt.Printf("Error parsing environment variable %s: %v\n",
		flagName, err)
		return defaultValue
	}

	return result
}
```

Here is an example of feature toggling in Golang. In the example, we have two boolean flags – **`feature-a`** and **`feature-b`**. The function **`getEnvBool`** dynamically checks the value of a flag using environment variables. The same check can be made by an API request to a third-party service. In the **`main`** function, we ask for the value of the flags and then determine whether to execute the business logic.

We can create a feature toggling external service by ourselves, or, more recommended is to use widely used SaaS like LaunchDarkly.

Rollouts

While deploying applications and services to production, the friction point of switching between the previous and new versions is called rollout. There are several techniques for performing a rollout, and all of them can be implemented in Kubernetes by using its native utilities or external software suitable for Kubernetes. Let's observe the different techniques.

Basic Deployment

This is the most straightforward way to perform rollout. It immediately kills all the previous instances (Pods) and creates new instances (Pods) with the new version. This technique is the fastest and most cost-effective way to perform rollout, although it is highly vulnerable to outages and has the highest risk. In Kubernetes, we can specify this technique to the workload by defining **`.spec.strategy.type==Recreate`**.

Rolling Update

Rolling Update allows the gradual rollout of new versions. We control the transition dose between the old and the new versions. Rolling Update starts new instances (Pods) of the new version and transfers traffic to them before the old version is terminated.

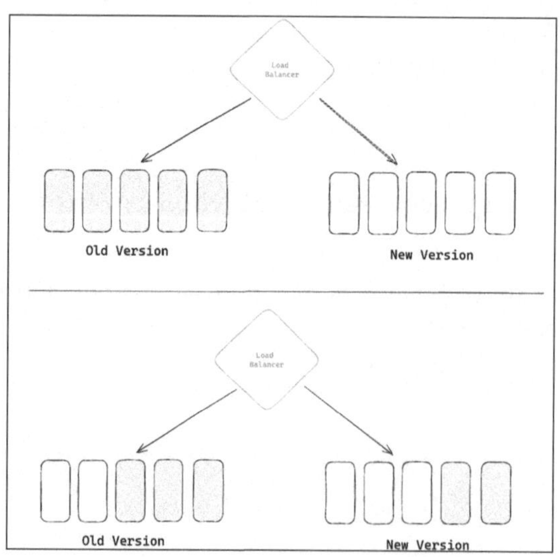

Figure 9.6: *Rolling Deployment*

To implement this type of rollout in Kubernetes, we need to specify the following configuration: **`.spec.strategy.type==RollingUpdate`**. Things that can be adjusted while performing a rolling update supported in Kubernetes can be:

- **Max Unavailable:** Maximum number of Pods that can be unavailable during rollout. It can be an absolute number (5, for example) or a percentage (70%).
- **Max Surge:** Maximum number of Pods that can be created above the desired number (of Pods) defined in the workload. Like the previous configuration, it can be an absolute number or percentage.

Blue-Green Deployment

This is the safest rollout technique, allowing the creation of the desired new version with all the instances (Pods). By making a manual decision, the developer can choose whether to route the network to the old version (blue in the following figure) or the new version (green in the following figure).

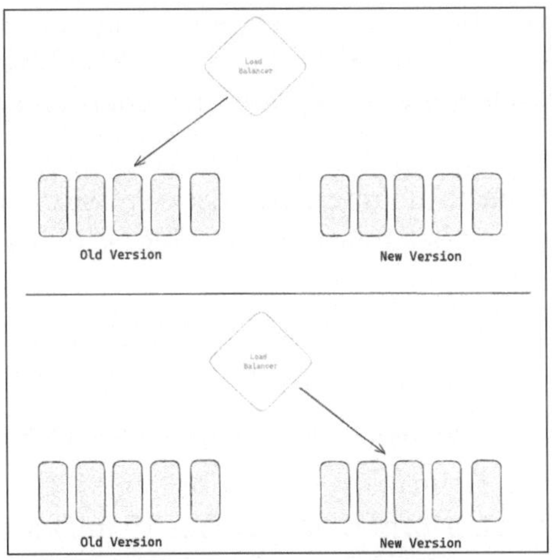

Figure 9.7: *Blue-Green Deployment*

There aren't built-in solutions to run Blue-Green Deployment in Kubernetes. However, there are tools like ArgoCD that allow us to do so. In general, Blue/Green Deployment refers to creating all the desired software (even the entire system) and then deciding which version to route all the network traffic. Although it is the safest way to perform rollout, it is the least cost-effective technique and takes the maximum time.

Multi-Service Rollout

This rollout technique refers to rolling out from the system point of view and not from a single service point of view. Using Multi-Services Rollout, we'll want to rollout several services together as a single unit. We can use any technique that we mentioned before to perform Multi-Service Rollout. Kubernetes doesn't offer built-in capability to perform this technique. However, Helm is one of the most popular native Kubernetes open-source tools in the market, and it allows one to do so very quickly. Helm, an open-source templating engine for Kubernetes used to manage charts, can aggregate several Kubernetes resources and roll out all of them at once.

Canary Deployment

Canary Deployment is a combination of Rolling Update and Blue-Green Deployment. This technique allows us to perform a gradual rollout like the Rolling Update technique, simultaneously routing traffic to both the old and the new versions. Like the Blue-Green Deployment, the Canary Deployment allows us to observe the two versions and manually decide whether to route all the traffic to the new version or keep routing traffic to the previous version. Like Blue-Green Deployment, it doesn't have a built-in solution in Kubernetes, and we can use external tools like ArgoCD.

Rollbacks

A new version often won't be as we expected and might cause several issues and failures. In such cases, we wish to perform a Rollback. Rollback is reverting a system or application to a previous state or version. In Kubernetes, there are two ways to perform rollback:

- **Kubectl**: Each resource in Kubernetes has a revision, and each time we roll out a new version, it creates a new revision. Here is how we can perform rollback using `kubectl` for example:

  ```
  kubectl rollout undo <kind>/<resource-name> --to-revision=<revi-
  sion-number>
  ```

  ```
  kubectl rollout undo deployment/nginx-deployment --to-revision=2
  ```

- **Helm**: Each chart in Helm has reversion because it is a resource in Kubernetes. Here is how we can perform rollback using Helm, for example:

  ```
  helm rollback <RELEASE> [REVISION] [flags]
  ```

  ```
  helm rollback frontend-services 13
  ```

Conclusion

In this chapter, we explored the critical steps necessary to prepare our applications and services for deployment to production. From the initial code completion to ensuring that our service is production-ready, we covered various topics, including CI/CD, design for failure, timeouts, retries, fallback mechanisms, and security measures such as authentication and authorization.

We delved into various deployment strategies, such as basic deployment, rolling updates, blue-green deployment, canary deployment, and multi-service rollout, each with its own advantages and considerations. Furthermore, we discussed the importance of feature toggling as a technique to gradually introduce new features and the concept of rollbacks to revert to a previous stable version in case of unexpected issues.

Through practical examples, especially in the context of Golang, we demonstrated how to implement these techniques effectively. By understanding and applying these concepts, developers can ensure that their services are delivered to production as anticipated and maintain their integrity and reliability in the face of potential failures.

As we conclude this chapter, it's clear that deploying applications to production is a multifaceted process that requires careful planning and execution. By adhering to best practices and leveraging the tools and techniques discussed, developers can confidently navigate the complexities of production deployment and ensure the success of their services in the real world.

In *Chapter 10, Next Steps in Production*, we'll cover what to consider while our application and service are already in production.

References

- https://www.mabl.com/blog/what-is-cicd
- https://github.com/sony/gobreaker
- https://aws.amazon.com/blogs/containers/building-a-fault-tolerant-architecture-with-a-bulkhead-pattern-on-aws-app-mesh/
- https://github.com/remeh/sizedwaitgroup
- https://www.okta.com/identity-101/authentication/
- https://www.okta.com/identity-101/authentication-vs-authorization/
- https://launchdarkly.com
- https://codefresh.io/learn/software-deployment/
- https://kubernetes.io/docs/concepts/workloads/controllers/deployment/#rolling-update-deployment
- https://argo-cd.readthedocs.io/en/stable/
- https://github.com/helm/helm

CHAPTER 10
Next Steps in Production

Introduction

This chapter will focus on aspects we must consider while our services operate in production. A service that is now stable and operating in production doesn't mean it will keep operating correctly. Production services left unattended are like neglected gardens – they wither over time. Many things are changing under our noses – new vulnerabilities discovered, new customers bringing new cases we didn't experience, scaling effects, and so on. Maintenance is the lifeline of resilience!

Maintenance does not only include the bugs and issues in the code. It includes culture. A good culture will solve issues faster without blaming a specific person for the problem.

Maintenance includes observing the systems and monitoring what is happening through telemetry. Telemetry data can be logs, metrics, and tracing. We should strive to have observability, which will allow us to gain control over our system. When we observe a problem or bug, we'll want to solve it and seek a solution - troubleshooting. This chapter will dive into the troubleshooting process and what is included inside.

When using a microservices system, the power of distributed maintenance is crucial, and without it, the microservices architecture is much less powerful.

Structure

In this chapter, we will discuss the following topics:

- Monitoring
- Observability
    - Logs
    - Metrics
    - Tracing

- Production Troubleshooting
    - The Power of Theory
- Profiling
    - PGO
    - Performance Issues
- Alerting
    - Performance Metrics

Monitoring

Monitoring allows stakeholders to deeply understand how remote environments work, such as production or staging. It is the continuous process of observing, collecting, and analyzing data on a system's performance, health, and behavior. This ensures the system operates well and as expected.

Monitoring **continuously observes** and analyzes the performance, health, and availability of applications, infrastructure, and services to detect and respond to real-time issues and ensure optimal operation. It involves collecting metrics, logs, and other data to provide insights into the system's behavior and identify potential problems or improvements.

Monitoring helps us detect trends and anomalies across the system and services. By setting predefined thresholds and conditions for data that interest us, we can define alerts or notifications based on monitoring.

Usually, we can view the monitoring output through dashboards explaining what is happening.

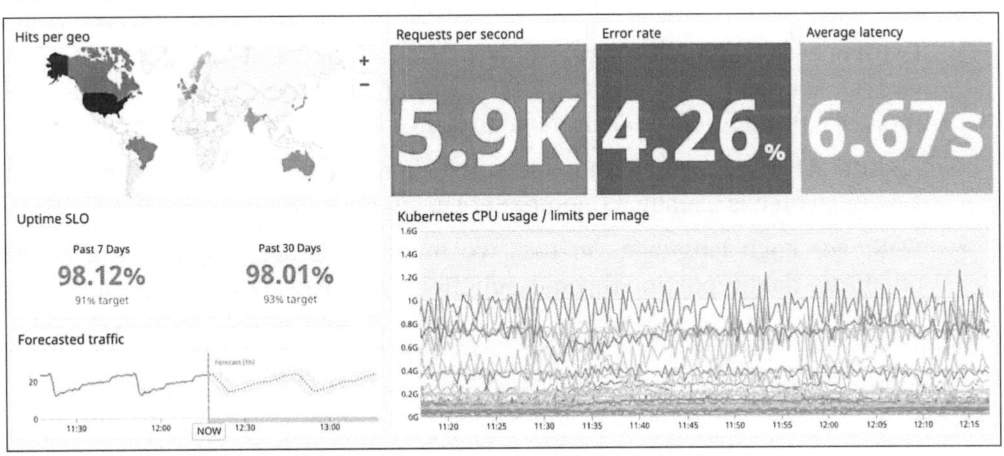

Figure 10.1: *Monitoring Dashboard Example*

The preceding figure shows an example of a monitoring dashboard.

Monitoring and APM are concepts that are often used interchangeably. APM, which stands for Application Performance Monitoring, is a subset of monitoring used to track a specific application's performance. APM tracks whether the application is stable and available, as well as error rate, latency, and so on. Monitoring is a broader topic that can describe things other than performance, like trends, number of paying customers, geographic specification data, SLO (service level objective), and more. Examples of famous monitoring tools in the market are Prometheus, DataDog, and NewRelic.

Observability

Observability is the ability to measure the current state of a system and aggregate all the data into a historical view. Observability uses three types of telemetry data - logs, metrics, and tracing. This is also the historical order in which they were introduced.

We can refer to observability as a system property, like functionality or testability.

Observability lets us understand **why and how** the system behavior is as it is, which differs from monitoring, which lets us understand **what** is happening through analysis.

We'll use the power of observability to solve real and potential problems. Without observability, we can't maintain our system and can't perform troubleshooting, which will be discussed later in this chapter.

A good analogy for telling the difference between monitoring and observability is to treat our system as a patient. Monitoring is like viewing a patient's vital signs (heartbeat, blood pressure, temperature, injuries, and others). On the other end, to heal the patient, we need to look at his historical medical issues and investigate specific theories regarding why he is ill.

When deploying microservices architecture, we must create a monitoring system. Creating a monitoring system while using Kubernetes includes three parts:

- **Centralized Monitoring System:** A unified platform aggregating data from various sources, providing tools for viewing and analyzing. We can use OSS tools like Prometheus and Grafana or SaaS tools like DataDog and NewRelic.
- **Agents:** They report all the telemetry data to the centralized monitoring system, which is usually a DaemonSet sitting on each node.
- **SDK:** For each language we use, we must implement logic that supports telemetry data reporting through functions, middlewares, and so on.

Let's explore the three telemetry data types.

Logs

Logs are records of events, actions, or messages a software application or system generates for troubleshooting, monitoring, and analysis. Logs can be used to give information and report warnings or errors. With logs, we can understand **what**

happened and when it happened, like leaving breadcrumbs in the code. Logs should be composed in human-readable JSON format and not just plain text, although this is an option. Log comprises metadata (date, service, and so on), log level, and the log itself. Usually, the log metadata is injected into the log manually or during the usage of the SDK. Here are the common log levels:

- **Info:** Useful information; usually, we don't care too much about them. It is typically the default log level.
- **Debug:** This log is intended for logging information details for debugging purposes. It will be deleted sometime in the future.
- **Warning:** Anything that can potentially cause errors in the system. It can be delays, high latency, and so on. These kinds of logs never require immediate remediation.
- **Error:** This log indicates something terrible happened and usually requires user intervention. It usually requires immediate attention.
- **Fatal:** An error that forces the service to go down or restart. It is an extreme situation that will require an instant reaction.

Here are a few examples of logs:

- `[INFO] User was logged into the system. { "name": "John", "company": "Nick"}`
- `[DEBUG] Query was executed. { "query": "SELECT * FROM accounts", "execution_time": "15s"}`
- `[WARNING] Event took a lot of time to proceed. { "event_id": "12345", "time": "30s"}`
- `[ERROR] Unable to connect to the external API. Retrying in 2 seconds.`
- `[FATAL] Server got panic. Shutting down the application`

One of Golang's core packages is **`"log"`**, which contains log functionality. An alternative with more advanced options is the package - **`"github.com/sirupsen/logrus"`**.

Metrics

A metric is a quantitative measurement represented as a data point. Metrics can include tags. Tags represent metadata on the metric; examples include account name, user name, environment, app version, and so on. We can build graphs in different layout forms in any monitoring system based on the metrics data points over time. We can also create partition graphs using the metrics tags and defined aggregated time durations of the metrics.

There are a variety of metrics types. Here, we'll mention the three leading types.

- **Counter:** This cumulative metric represents a value that can increase or be restarted to zero. Examples of metrics of a counter can be the number of failed requests, the number of total requests, the amount of users that used the system, and so on.

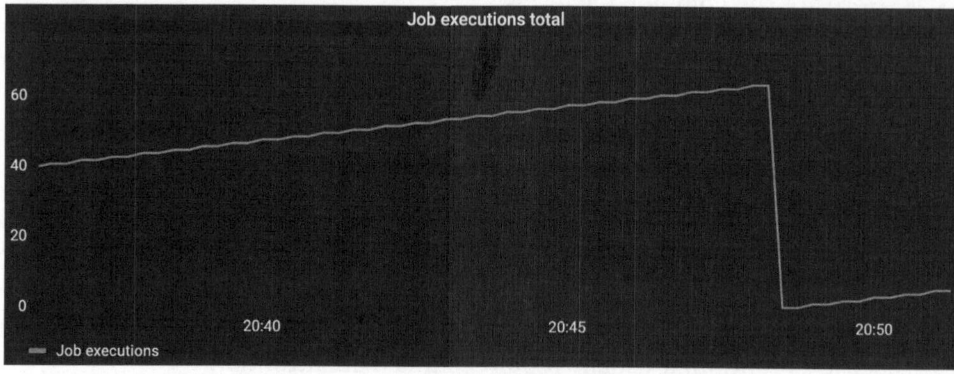

Figure 10.2: *Counter Metric example of "Job execution total"*

- **Gauge:** A single number metric representing an arbitrary value that can go up or down. Examples of gauge metrics include temperature, CPU usage, memory usage, and the number of active users.
- **Histogram:** A metric that samples observations and counts the observations in buckets. For example, a histogram can measure latency, request size, task duration, and so on.

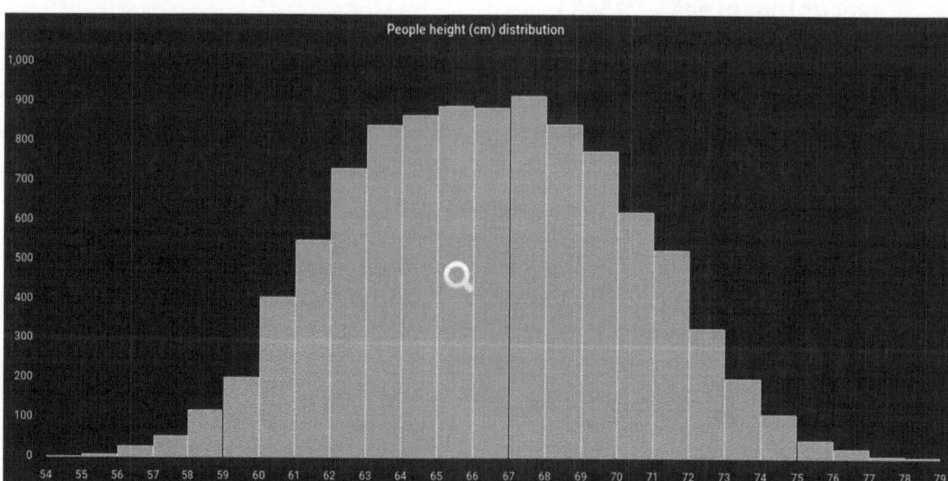

Figure 10.3: *Histogram Metric example of People's Height (cm)*

Tracing

Trace is a newer telemetry than log and metric. It gives a much more comprehensive view of the application. Trace's goal is to follow the application's flow, whether data propagation or request flow, which is relevant for RESTful API services in a microservices architecture due to the frequent request rate. Tracing allows us to see the flow of functions from start to end, which function invokes which function/s, the duration of each function, the parameters passed between them, metadata about each step, and more. Each step is inside a trace called a span. The entire trace can tell a user's story and what happened to him along the way.

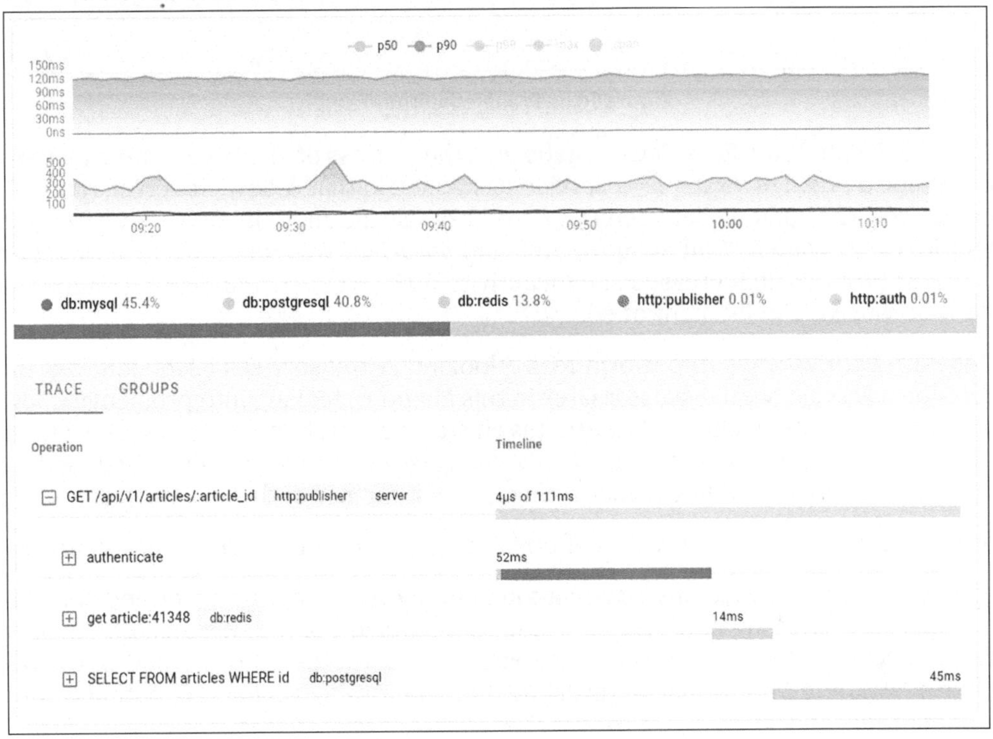

Figure 10.4: *Tracing Example*

In the preceding figure, we can see an example of a trace. The trace aims to track and endpoint **`GET /api/v1/articles/:article_id`**. In the trace, we can see three spans - **`authenticate, get article:41348, SELECT FROM articles WHERE id`**. For each span, we can see duration, the order of the spans, and other data not shown in the figure. A more advanced tracing capability is to perform distributed tracing. This involves performing a wide trace instead of a trace inside a single application, a single trace across many services.

Production Troubleshooting

Production troubleshooting is a systematic process of taking immediate action to remediate the issue to return the system to a healthy state, performing RCA, and resolving the root cause to prevent the same problem from occurring again. Let's break this process of troubleshooting.

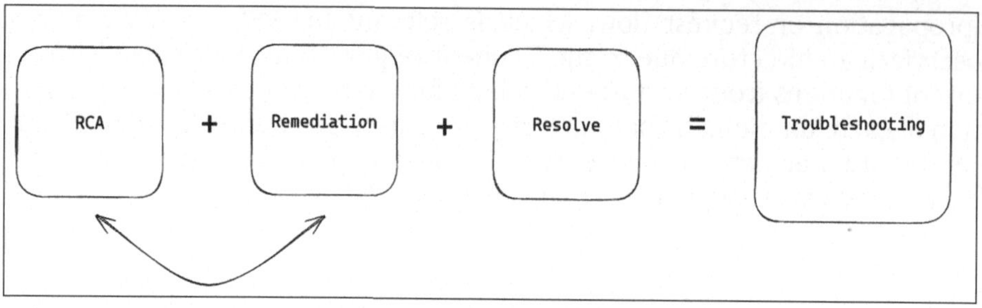

Figure 10.5: *Troubleshooting Parts*

RCA, which stands for **Root Cause Analysis**, is the process of identifying the underlying reason for a bug. For example, a service has a metric that follows its error rate for a month, and the value is between 0.1% and 0.2% all the time. Immediately after a PR (Pull Request) named "*Changing the API configuration*" was deployed to production, the error rate metric increased significantly to 50%. We can confidently assume that the root cause is the PR mentioned.

There are various ways to perform RCA - looking at the services dashboard, putting alerts on a service (we'll discuss it later in this chapter), looking into problematic logs, looking at the system metrics, Kubernetes cluster metrics, Kubernetes logs, describing the service' Pods in Kubernetes, CI/CD changes, downtime of third-party service, anomaly detection, profiling (which we'll discuss it further in this chapter), and so on.

Remediation refers to the process of preventing a current bad state from occurring.

Until we have performed any remediation action, our system isn't working correctly or, worse, not working at all. Such a situation is called P0. The Remediation process can be performed in several ways: Rollback in Kubernetes, as described in *Chapter 8, Introduction to Microservices*, reverting a PR, increasing replicas, updating expired configuration, and so on.

Sometimes, we don't have to perform full RCA to perform remediation, which can be partial. For example, if we indicated a bad PR, the remediation action is probably to revert it, although we don't know what was inside the PR that caused the bug.

Resolve refers to the process of preventing the lousy state from occurring again. By understanding the root cause of the issue, we can take preventive actions. Examples of resolve actions- fixing a bug through debugging, tweaking API/DB configuration, increasing replica amount, and so on. Note that the remediation action is sometimes the same as the resolve action.

The Power of Theory

There is no theory without observability and vice versa.

We already discussed observability, but let's discuss theory and explain the preceding statement. A theory is an idea that explains the existing data: why do the graphs look the way they are stacked and not the other way around? For example, we can see a graph of ongoing increments in memory usage, which can be explained by memory leaks.

To illustrate the relationship between **theory** and **observability,** we'll give an analogy from Reference number 5.

Is a doctor with extensive knowledge about the human body and always up to date with the latest medical news a good doctor? The answer is no unless the doctor can test the patient and get data about him. Without proper testing of the patient, he won't be able to serve the appropriate treatments, and every treatment without data will be a guess.

On the other hand, you are an average person without a fundamental understanding of the human body. Still, you have the latest technology for testing patients and all the patient data. Are you a good doctor? The answer is no unless you have fundamental knowledge about the human body.

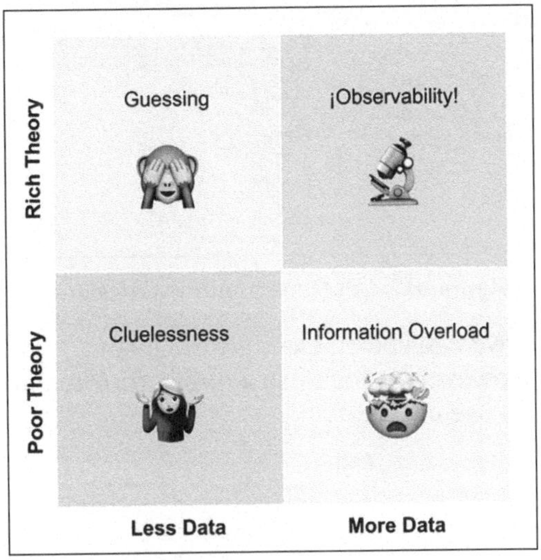

Figure 10.6: *Observability and Theory*

The analogy of a doctor is moral to a developer, the theory is moral to the doctor's knowledge, and data is moral to data. Without a rich theory based on software knowledge and internal business knowledge on the one hand and data on the other hand, we can't gain observability.

Each time we start troubleshooting or performing RCA, we should keep some theory in mind regarding the root cause and validate the theory against the data, or looking at the data will lead us to consolidate another theory that we can validate.

Profiling

Profiling analyzes a program in runtime to measure metrics like execution time, CPU usage, memory usage, goroutines running, and more. Profiling allows us to identify bottlenecks, improve performance, and optimize code efficiency. Usually, using third-party tools like Grafana or DataDog will create a flame graph. Although there are other ways to view profiling data.

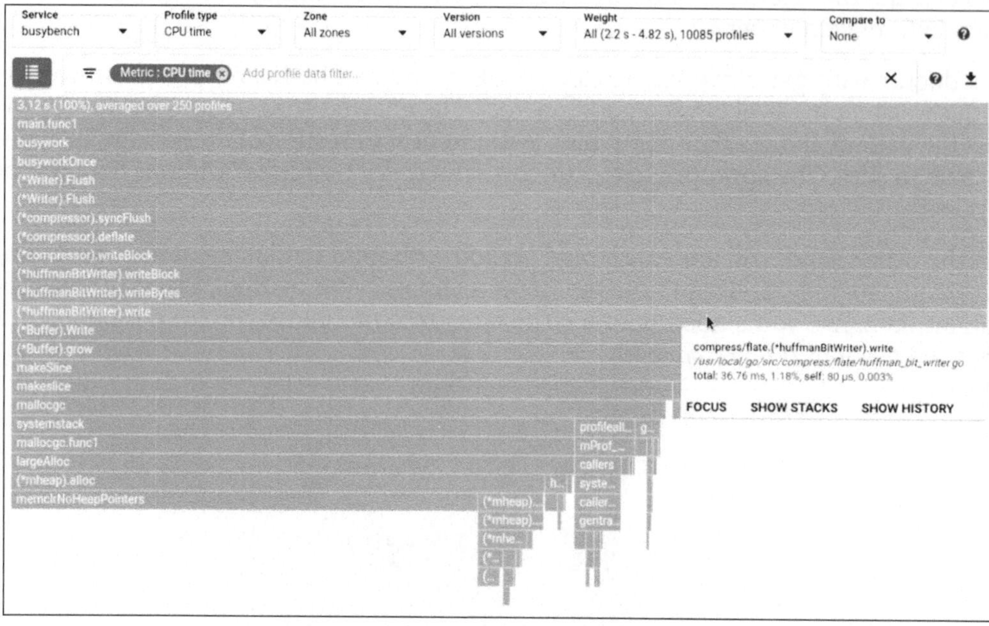

Figure 10.7: *CPU time profiling flame graph*

In the preceding figure, we can see an example of Golang application profiling of CPU time in Google Cloud. However, we can use a native tool invented by the Golang team - **pprof**. Let's see how to use it:

```
package main

import (
	"net/http"
	_ "net/http/pprof"
	"sync"
	"time"
)

var leakSlice1 = []string{}
var leakSlice2 = []string{}
var leakSlice3 = []string{}
```

```
func main() {
	// start pprof server
	go func() {
		http.ListenAndServe(":6060", nil)
	}()

	wg := sync.WaitGroup{}
	wg.Add(1)
	go leak(&wg)
	wg.Wait()
}

func leak(wg *sync.WaitGroup) {
	defer wg.Done()
	for i := 0; i < 10_000_000; i++ {
		appendToLeakSlice1()
		if (i % 10_000) == 0 {
			time.Sleep(100 * time.Millisecond)
		}
	}
}

func appendToLeakSlice1() {
	leakSlice1 = append(leakSlice1, "a")
	appendToLeakSlice2()
}

func appendToLeakSlice2() {
	leakSlice2 = append(leakSlice2, "ab")
	appendToLeakSlice3()
}
```

```
func appendToLeakSlice3() {
	leakSlice3 = append(leakSlice3, "abc")
}
```

In the preceding example, all we needed to start the profile was:

- Importing the **pprof** package by declaring: `_ "net/http/pprof"` .
- Start a goroutine in some port:

```
go func() {
    http.ListenAndServe(":6060", nil)
}()
```

The code after that is there to demonstrate the memory usage of the program. To look at the memory usage, we can use the Golang CLI:

```
go tool pprof -web http://localhost:6060/debug/pprof/heap
```

The **-web** flag opens the memory in a nice UI. We don't need to use it.

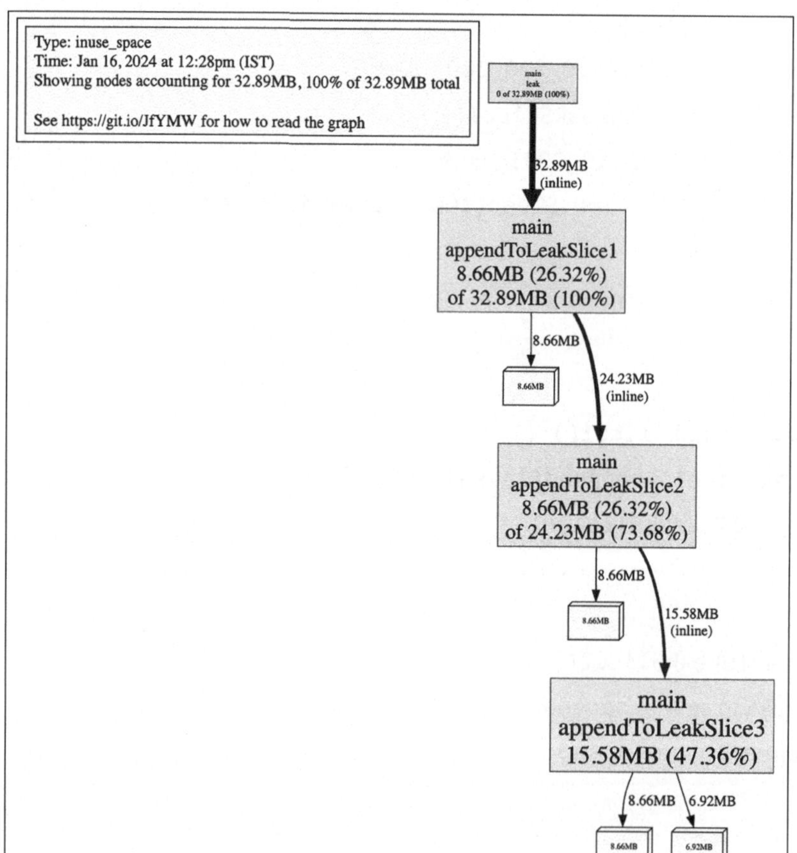

Figure 10.8: *pprof heap usage*

After a few seconds, the memory heap glanced differently.

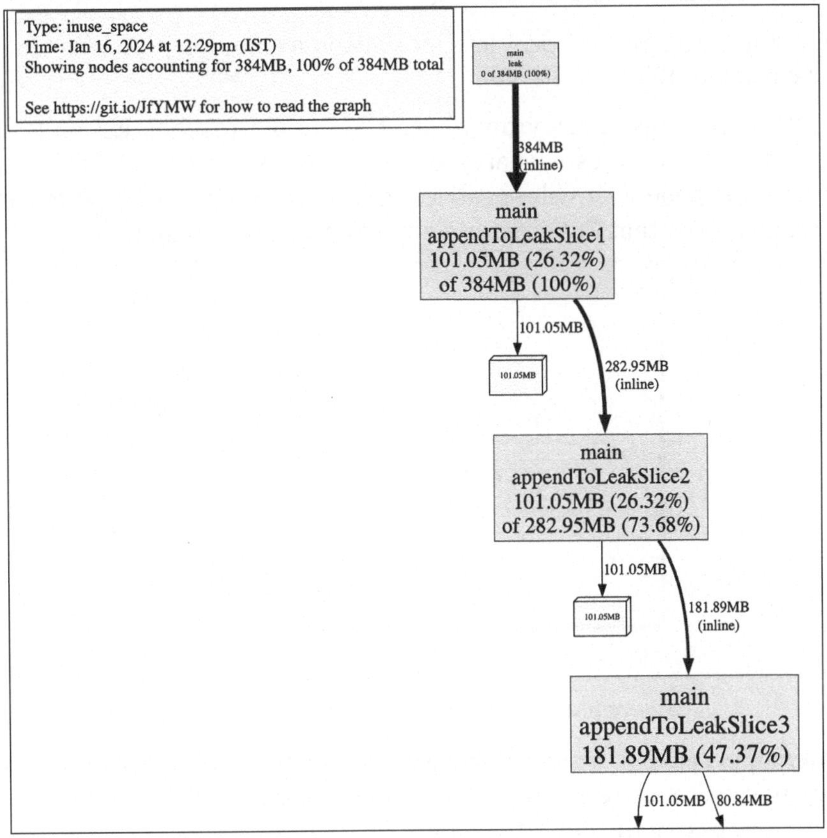

Figure 10.9: *pprof heap usage 2*

Let's not focus on the data within the preceding two figures. The purpose of bringing them is to illustrate the power of the **pprof** package in Golang and how we can use it. Rather than seeing the memory distribution among functions in runtime, we can also look at metrics like CPU and goroutines execution. To look further into those options, look at - **https://pkg.go.dev/net/http/pprof**. Using `pprof` is pretty straightforward when understanding the usage for one metric (like the `heap` metric we presented in this section).

PGO

Profile-**G**uided **O**ptimization is a compiler optimization method that uses the information from profiling to leverage it for optimizations. The compiler will generate high-performance binary code using this profiling data (**pprof** output). PGO is available in Golang from version 1.21. Whenever building Golang code, it will seek for **default.pgo** file, which contains profiling information. Another way is to specify a specific profiling file **go build -pgo=/tmp/foo.pprof**. We won't dive into the process of using PGO; our goal is to know about the existence of this method.

Performance Issues

Before jumping to the next section, let's look at some common performance issues we can resolve using profiling:

- **CPU Throttling**: A scenario where CPU usage reaches its limits. This is a standard Kubernetes scenario, once we reach a Pod's CPU limit. Once this scenario happens, it will negatively affect the application's performance and stability. Note that Kubernetes won't restart the container.

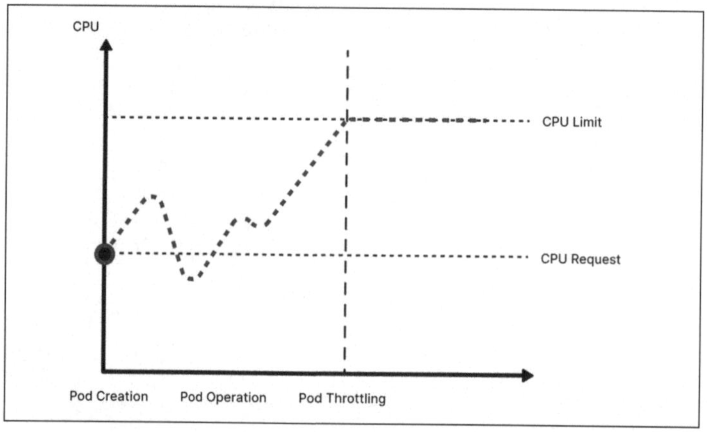

Figure 10.10: *CPU Throttling of Pod in Kubernetes*

- **Memory Leak**: A scenario where the application consistently consumes memory without releasing it. In Kubernetes, the Pod will be restarted if the memory passes the limit threshold.

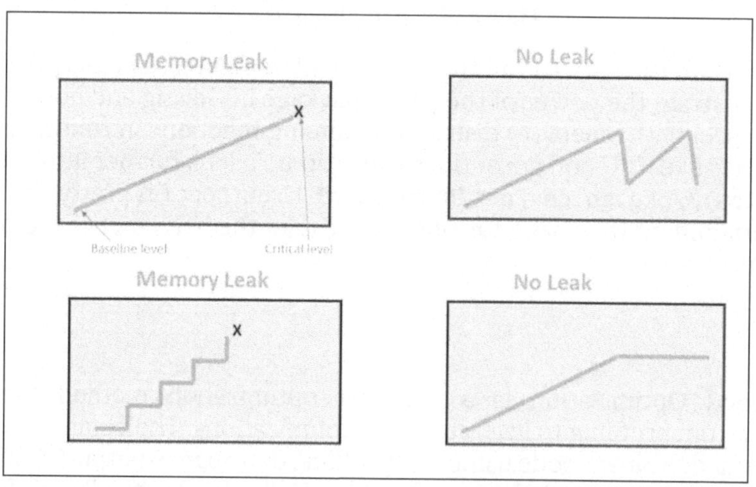

Figure 10.11: *Memory Leaks Types*

The two left graphs show a scenario where a memory leak can occur - if the application is consuming the memory and never releases it or stabilized (top-left), don't be confused from the bottom right graph. In that graph, the application consumes an essential memory and then stabilizes. There is much to discuss about memory leaks; however, this book won't discuss it more.

- **Goroutine Leak:** We already discussed this topic in *Chapter* 5, *Unlocking* Go's *Concurrency Power*. The **pprof** package also allows us to track the amount and distribution of goroutines in Golang.

Alerting

We deployed the services to production and monitored our services' performance and behavior; we also built a neat dashboard that will give us observability regarding all the APIs and their communication. All that is great. Unfortunately, we aren't always near computers, and sometimes AFK (aka for Away From Keyboard). However, a system is a living creature that always operates; we must take care of it when we aren't nearby. To align with our desired performance, we must put an alert that will notify us when needed.

An alert is a signal generated by an automated monitoring system, determining thresholds that are supposed to provide information for critical issues. This information is necessary to preserve a system's health and performance.

Popular alerting systems are PagerDuty and Atlassian Opsgenie. Those systems have advanced escalation functionality like sending messages via Slack, email, SMS, or even phone calls. We can configure whom to direct the alert to at a particular moment by specifying the OnCall schedule.

Performance Metrics

These are recommended performance metrics for an RESTful API. We should monitor and alert if some threshold is being exceeded:

- **Requests Success Rate**: The percentage of requests that didn't experience errors out of all the requests. For example, two requests failed out of 1000 requests - the success rate is 99.8%. In systems where each decimal point represents a lot of users, it is common to measure performance with the number of 9s. For example, a success rate of 99.9992% is five times 9s. Each request is classified to a boolean parameter to determine if the request was a success or failure, regardless of the latency. Usually, only 5XX errors are classified as failure. This metric indicates how many users experienced bad journeys using your applications.
- **P95 Latency**: P95 stands for the 95th percentile. This metric reveals that 95% of the request duration was under this metric value. For example, if P95 is 0.5 seconds, 95% of the requests' latency was under 0.5 seconds.
- **P99 Latency**: This is the same as the previous metric but for the 99th percentile. Both metrics help ensure that the vast majority of the users are

experiencing a good journey using the APIs or applications. We don't want to measure the average because of average flooding anomalies that don't reflect the real user experience. Note that when measuring these metrics, we only consider success requests.

Conclusion

This final chapter explored the crucial aspects of maintaining services in a production environment. We emphasized that a stable service in production requires continuous attention and maintenance to remain resilient.

We delved into the importance of observability achieved through telemetry data like logs, metrics, and tracing. This observability allows us to monitor our systems, detect anomalies, and troubleshoot issues effectively. We also discussed various strategies for handling production troubleshooting, including the power of theory, profiling, and using Profile-Guided Optimization (PGO) for performance enhancements.

Furthermore, we covered the significance of alerting systems to notify us of critical issues when we are not actively monitoring our services. Lastly, we outlined some recommended performance metrics for RESTful APIs to ensure a positive user experience.

What's Next?

- **Deep Dive into Observability Tools:** Explore advanced features and capabilities of observability tools like Prometheus, Grafana, and Jaeger.
- **Advanced Troubleshooting Techniques:** Develop skills in advanced troubleshooting techniques, including distributed tracing and chaos engineering, to proactively identify and resolve potential problems.
- **Performance Optimization:** Focus on performance optimization strategies, including profiling and tuning, to enhance the efficiency and scalability of your services.
- **Security Best Practices:** Delve into security best practices for microservices, including encryption, access control, and regular security audits, to protect your services from threats and vulnerabilities.

By mastering these areas, you can ensure the continued reliability, performance, and security of your services in production, ultimately leading to a more robust and resilient system.

References

- https://www.comparitech.com/net-admin/solarwinds-npm-vs-datadog/
- https://blog.danslimmon.com/2019/05/03/no-observability-without-theory/

- https://levelup.gitconnected.com/prometheus-counter-metrics-d6c393d86076
- https://grafana.com/docs/grafana/latest/fundamentals/intro-histograms/
- https://blog.danslimmon.com/2019/05/03/no-observability-without-theory/
- https://cloud.google.com/profiler/docs/interacting-flame-graph
- https://www.airplane.dev/blog/kubernetes-cpu-limits-and-throttling
- https://medium.com/@shivam2003/memory-leak-unveiling-the-dark-side-of-c-the-silent-killer-lurking-in-your-code-e675599add9

Index

G